Visit our How To website at www.howto.co.uk

At **www.howto.co.uk** you can engage in conversation with our authors – all of whom have 'been there and done that' in their specialist fields. You can get access to special offers and additional content, but most importantly you will be able to engage with, and become a part of, a wide and growing community of people just like yourself.

At **www.howto.co.uk** you'll be able to talk and share tips with people who have similar interests and are facing similar challenges in their lives. People who, just like you, have the desire to change their lives for the better – be it through moving to a new country, starting a new business, growing their own vegetables, or writing a novel.

At **www.howto.co.uk** you'll find the support and encouragement you need to help make your aspirations a reality.

You can go direct to www.good-home-baking.co.uk, which is part of the main How To site.

How To Books strives to present authentic, inspiring, practical information in its books. Now, when you buy a title from **How To Books,** you get even more than just words on a page.

Good Home
BAKING

How to make your own delicious cakes,
biscuits, pastries and breads

DIANA PEACOCK

SPRING HILL

Published by Spring Hill, an imprint of How To Books Ltd.
Spring Hill House, Spring Hill Road
Begbroke, Oxford OX5 1RX
United Kingdom
Tel: (01865) 375794
Fax: (01865) 379162
info@howtobooks.co.uk
www.howtobooks.co.uk

How To Books greatly reduce the carbon footprint of their books
by sourcing their typesetting and printing in the UK.

The paper used for this book is FSC certified and totally chlorine-free. FSC (The Forest Stewardship Council) is an
international network to promote responsible management of the world's forests.

Text © 2010 Diana Peacock
Photographs © 2009 www.fabfoodpix.com

British Library Cataloguing in Publication Data
A catalogue record of this book is available from the British Library.

ISBN: 978 1 905862 42 9

Produced for How To Books by Deer Park Productions, Tavistock, Devon
Designed and typeset by Mousemat Design Ltd
Edited by Jamie Ambrose
Printed and bound by in Great Britain by Ashford Colour Press Ltd, Gosport, Hants

NOTE: The material contained in this book is set out in good faith for general guidance and no liability can be
accepted for loss or expense incurred as a result of relying in particular circumstances on statements made in the book.
Laws and regulations are complex and liable to change, and readers should check the current position with relevant
authorities before making personal arrangements.

Contents

For Millicent, Leslie and Trevor Sutton, with love.

Introduction

Bread and cake of all kinds have been an important part of our diet throughout history. Simple types of breads, cakes and biscuits were made by the ancient Egyptians and Greeks – although they were nothing like the baked items we know today. For one thing, dough was sweetened with honey for centuries; we didn't start using sugar until the 1700s. In addition, baking powder wasn't known about until around 1850, when Alfred Bird (of custard-powder fame) discovered that using baking soda and an edible acid together made bread or cake rise successfully without yeast.

Today, however, baking wonderful homemade cakes and bread has never been easier. With widely available good-quality ingredients, there is almost no end to the possible recipes.

Why bake your own?

Making your own bread, cakes, biscuits and pastries has many benefits. For one thing, there is the pride and contentment you feel when you have home-baked something successfully. The taste and quality are so much better than shop-bought because you don't add preservatives or colour enhancers. Best of all is, you know exactly what you have used in your baking – there are no secrets.

Baking is also important to culture and society because it is so closely associated with ceremonies and religious festivals of all kinds. From harvest loaves to simnel cakes, the reasons for baking many items are historical; and even if the original reasons have been forgotten, the traditions still occupy a well-loved place on our tables.

Similarly, families also have recipes that have been passed down through generations to become traditions – even if it is only baking that special cake for when other family members come and visit.

Where should you start?

If the home-baking process is completely new to you, it's best to start with something easy. Scones, for example (see page 132), are very simple, and if you make a ring of scones there isn't even any rolling out to be done; the whole process from start to first bite needn't take more than 30 minutes. Once you've mastered a few basics, you'll soon have your own favourites, and may even start experimenting and making up your own recipes. For this reason, you'll find a blank 'My Notes' page at the end of each chapter where you can jot down ingredients changes or recipe ideas. These, in turn, could very well become the next favourites that are passed down through the generations in your own family.

1
Baking Basics

Baking in all its forms is a great pleasure. Even if you have some disasters, they won't matter – after all, it's part of the learning process!

Bread and cakes, biscuits, scones and muffins are all popular items to make at home. Once you start baking, you will find that shop-bought products taste inferior to your own – and are overpriced. Obviously some commercially prepared baked items will always be hard to resist; I adore my local baker's vanilla slices and crispy dinner cobs. But many cakes and loaves on the shelves of supermarkets are nothing when compared with your own.

To speed you on the way to successful baking, then, here are some tips, ingredients and utensils that will help with your recipes. Don't, however, go out and buy everything at once; build it up slowly, according to what you need. Soon you will be eager to try all the baking techniques, but for now, just enjoy getting used to the basics.

Ingredients

Good-quality ingredients are necessary to produce good results. I have used all kinds of makes of flour, for example, from very expensive down to basic supermarket brands. The results have been more or less the same – although I do sift cheaper flour twice before using it in cakes. Try them yourself and see which you prefer and whether you notice any difference.

Flour You will work with three main types when baking. These include:

- *Plain*
  Suitable for biscuits and pastry. There is no raising agent in plain flour, but it may be used in conjunction with baking powder to make cakes and scones that require a raising agent. Comes in brown and wholemeal varieties.

- *Self-raising*
  This flour already contains baking powder so does exactly as its name suggests.

- *Strong*
  Suitable for bread-making and is explained in more detail in the chapter on bread-baking (see page 148). Comes in wholemeal, granary or brown.

Baking powder Usually a combination of baking soda and cream of tartar. It is combined with flour to aid rising and expansion.

Fat I always use butter, either slightly salted or unsalted, because the flavour is better than spreads. Always use butter at room temperature (or buy the spreadable version). A combination of lard and butter makes the best-flavoured and -textured shortcrust pastry. Oils can also be used in some cake or muffin recipes.

Sugar Finer sugar makes a lighter-textured cake, so caster sugar is usually better than granulated. Golden sugar or unrefined sugar gives a better flavour than white sugar. Soft-brown, light-brown and dark-brown sugars are useful have because they give a deeper colour and flavour to cakes, biscuits and sweetened bread. Icing sugar is used in many recipes for toppings and fillings.

Eggs Use the freshest eggs you can: this makes a big difference to the final flavour of your baking. Use whole eggs at room temperature for baking cakes, but if a recipe calls for yolks or whites, it is easier to separate a well-chilled egg; once the egg has been separated, allow it to reach room temperature before using. This will take about 45 minutes.

Dried fruit Raisins, sultanas, currants and glacé cherries are the most common, but dates, figs, cranberries, pineapple, apricots and apples are also useful. Having them in your cupboard means you can also make your own muesli.

Nuts Ground, chopped, flaked or whole, walnuts, hazelnuts, almonds, pecans and pistachios make for interesting ingredients. I probably use ground almonds more than any other in my recipes. Not only do they add texture and flavour, but they also keep a cake moist.

Milk This is often used as the liquid in baking, especially for cakes. Again, the rule is: the fresher, the better.

Dried yeast Used primarily for bread-making.

Jam A couple of different fruit preserves are good to keep on hand to use as pastry and cake fillings without any fuss or preparation.

Flavourings Don't be tempted to be buy synthetic flavourings; the aroma and taste of now widely available natural vanilla and almond extracts make a big difference to the flavour of your baking. You can also use the following:

- Coffee granules mixed with a little hot water make the best coffee flavouring around.
- Cocoa powder is used to give a chocolate flavour to cakes, biscuits and breads alongside real chocolate; the latter usually requires melting in a bowl over a pan of simmering water. An easier way is to use your microwave to melt the chocolate; this won't take long, however, so check your machine's instructions carefully.
- Lemon and orange zests are often used as flavouring, but be careful to take only the yellow or orange part and leave the creamy white pith as this is bitter. Use a zester or the fine side of your grater to scrape off the zest.

Herbs Dried herbs are a useful store-cupboard standby for many recipes to add flavour and interest to breads and scones. Parsley, sage, thyme, oregano, rosemary and tarragon are probably the most widely used.

Mustard powder/cayenne pepper Both of these add flavour and kick to savoury pastries, scones and muffins.

Salt and white and black pepper Must-haves.

Equipment

Just as the right ingredients are crucial to your recipes, having the right equipment on hand will help with your baking success.

Oven
All ovens vary, so when recipes give a cooking time, it is very approximate – always be aware of this. Cakes are affected by sudden drops in oven temperature and can sink if you open the oven door too soon. Always leave the cake for a recipe's shortest recommended time before checking it to avoid this.

Mixing bowls
Ideally, you should have two of these: a one big enough to hold a large mixture, such as a Christmas cake or bread dough, and a smaller one in which to mix icings and toppings.

Spoons
You need a couple of metal tablespoons and at least one wooden spoon. The wooden one is ideal for creaming and mixing bread dough, while metal tablespoons are best for folding in flour or egg whites, as the metal cuts through the mixture without letting air escape from it. You will also need a teaspoon to measure out ingredients in recipes.

Spatula
A plastic or silicone spatula is very useful for removing all the mixture from the mixing bowl so that none is wasted. It does the job with ease.

Scales
There are several ways to weigh out ingredients. There are balances, using brass or other metal weights; this is what I use. If using balances when weighing ingredients, the scales *must* balance – not weigh down heavier on the ingredients side. Other scales use a top bucket that allows for very accurate weighing by means of a dial or digital reading.

Electric whisks and mixers
A hand mixer is a must-have for me now; it speeds up creaming and mixing and is essential for making meringues. You still have instant control of the results, it is much easier than mixing by hand, and you can buy a good one for less than £15 nowadays. Food processors are also useful for preparing shortcrust pastry.

Jugs
Have a plastic and a glass measuring jug with easy-to-read millilitre amounts.

A small grater
For zesting fruit and grating nutmeg into recipes.

A large sieve
These come in plastic or metal; I have one of each.

Lining paper
Lining, baking or silicone paper is a coated paper suitable for lining cake tins and trays and is essential for baking meringues because they stick easily to other surfaces. Greaseproof paper also makes a good lining paper, but I still grease this anyway as it isn't always non-stick.

Cake and bread tins
Use as good-quality bakeware as you can afford; I have both metal and silicone. Non-stick types make it easier to turn out cakes and bread, but I still line non-stick tins with baking paper if making a cake unless I'm using a silicone tin – you don't even have to grease these. Springform or loose-bottomed tins also make it easier to remove the contents.

You will need a variety of baking tins in various shapes and sizes. A good selection for baking would include the following.

- Deep round tins suitable for large, deep cakes: 18cm, 20cm and 23cm.

- Round sandwich tins: 18cm and 20cm.

- Round springform tin: at least one 20cm, suitable for cheesecakes and tortes.

- Ring tins: for babas and sponge cakes; usually 20–23cm.

- Loaf tins: the most common size for most loaf cakes and bread is 23cm x 13cm x 7cm.

- Shallow rectangular tins: for slices and Swiss rolls, approximately 28cm x 18cm, or 30cm x 20cm.

- 12-hole bun tins and the larger muffin tins; one of each or two muffin-sized.

- Deep square tin: 20cm or 23cm, used for large cakes; this is especially good for birthday cakes.

- Baking trays: you need a couple of these in varying sizes for biscuits and pastries.

FILLINGS AND ICINGS

The right filling and icing add the finishing touches to your sweet bake goods, making them just that much more extra-special. On the following pages are some classic recipes that you will be able to turn to whenever you need them.

Classic Buttercream

80g butter
120g icing sugar
¼ teaspoon
vanilla extract

1. Cream the butter until light and fluffy.

2. Sift in the icing sugar and add the vanilla.

3. Beat until smooth and light.

Variations
• Sift 15g cocoa powder with the icing sugar for a simple chocolate-flavoured buttercream. Or try 20g drinking chocolate.

• Add the zest and 2 teaspoons of juice of either an orange, lemon or lime instead of vanilla extract for a citrusy buttercream.

• Add 1 level teaspoon of coffee granules to 3 teaspoons hot water, mix well, then beat this into the buttercream. Some recipes may call for a stronger coffee flavour but this is the basic one.

Glacé Icing

The shiny set topping used on buns and fairy cakes. Some cakes require a runnier icing that is drizzled over; this will be specified in the recipe.

100g icing sugar
Water to mix

1. Sift the sugar into a bowl.

2. Mix the water into the sugar a teaspoon at a time until the icing is just runny.

Royal Icing

The classic Christmas cake topping. It can be smoothed out using a damp palette knife, or you can rough it up artistically so that it resembles snow.

3 egg whites
500g icing sugar
1 teaspoon lemon juice

1. Put the egg whites into a mixing bowl.

2. Sift in 2 tablespoons of icing sugar at a time, beating as you go.

3. When the icing has reached a thick dropping consistency, add the lemon juice and beat until it forms stiff peaks.

4. Use immediately.

Fudge Icing

This is ideal to sandwich cakes together because it is less ultra-sweet than buttercream.

Covers a 23cm cake or 12 buns

50g butter
3 tablespoons
  evaporated milk
200g icing sugar,
  sifted well
½ teaspoon
  vanilla extract

1. Put the butter and evaporated milk in a pan and heat gently until the butter has melted. Remove from the heat.

2. Add the icing sugar 2 tablespoons at a time and stir in well after each addition, adding the vanilla at some point during the process.

3. Use when completely cool.

Variations
• For a chocolate version, add 30g cocoa powder to the icing sugar when sifting.

• For a coffee flavour add 1 teaspoon coffee granules to 3 teaspoons hot water and mix together. Add this as you stir in the sugar.

Cream Cheese Frosting

This rich, full-fat frosting is ideal for icing ginger and carrot cakes.

Covers a 20cm round cake

100g cream cheese
50g caster sugar
50g icing sugar
40g butter, softened
½ teaspoon
   vanilla extract

1. Beat the cream cheese until it is loose and soft, then add the sugars and beat in.

2. Add the butter and vanilla and beat lightly.

3. Use immediately.

Low-fat Cream Cheese Frosting

A much lighter topping for cakes than standard cream-cheese frosting.

100g low-fat soft
   cream cheese
50g caster sugar
50g icing sugar
50g low-fat
   crème fraîche
½ teaspoon
   vanilla extract

1. Beat the cheese to loosen it up, then add all the other ingredients.

2. Beat well until smooth and thick.

Marzipan

Marzipan is used to cover cakes before topping them with royal icing. It is also good for making stollen and Battenbergs, and the good news is that you can either use it immediately or store it until needed. Any leftovers may also be wrapped in cling film and foil or placed in a freezer bag and stored in the fridge for one week or frozen. Always bring marzipan back to room temperature before using.

Covers a 23cm round or 20cm square cake, a large Battenberg or fills 2 stollen loaves

200g caster sugar
200g icing sugar
400g ground almonds
2 eggs plus 1 egg yolk
2 teaspoons lemon juice
½ teaspoon
   almond extract

1. Put the caster sugar in a mixing bowl and sift in the icing sugar. Stir the two sugars together, then add the almonds and stir again.

2. Beat the egg yolk and whole eggs with the lemon juice and almond extract.

3. Make a well in the centre of the dry ingredients and stir in half of the egg mixture. Keep adding the egg mixture a little at a time until the marzipan is soft and pliable but not sticky.

4. Lightly dust a work surface with icing sugar and knead the marzipan until it becomes smooth and easy to handle.

Crème Pâtissière (Pastry Custard)

This is used instead of buttercream to fill sandwich cakes or vanilla slices. It also makes a good custard base for strawberry and other fruit flans.

Makes enough to fill a large sandwich cake or 4 large vanilla slices

250ml milk
2 tablespoons cornflour
3 egg yolks
2 tablespoons
  caster sugar
½ teaspoon
  vanilla extract

1. Reserve 3 tablespoons of the milk and put the rest in a pan and heat until it is warm. Remove from the heat.

2. Mix the reserved milk with the cornflour.

3. Whisk the egg yolks and sugar together in a separate bowl. Pour the warm milk into the egg mixture, whisking to combine, then stir in the vanilla.

4. Pour the custard back into the pan and stir in the cornflour paste. Mix in vigorously.

5. Heat on a low heat, whisking all the time, until the mixture comes to the boil.

6. Put a disc of baking parchment over the custard to stop a skin forming on the top. Allow to cool before using.

Chocolate Cream Custard

Use this luscious custard to fill cakes and pastries.

Makes enough for 1 large cake or 12 small eclairs

100ml milk
1½ tablespoon cornflour
150ml single cream
100g dark chocolate,
  broken into pieces
2 tablespoons
  caster sugar
3 egg yolks

1. Mix 3 tablespoons of the milk with the cornflour to make a thin paste.

2. Put the rest of the milk, cream and chocolate in a pan over a low heat. When the chocolate has melted, bring to the boil, then remove from the heat.

3. Beat the sugar and cornflour paste into the egg yolks, then stir this vigorously into the chocolate mixture.

4. Put back over a very low heat and stir until it thickens. Place a disc of greaseproof paper over the top to prevent a skin forming.

5. Cool completely before using.

FILLINGS AND ICINGS
My Notes

2
Simple Cakes and Sponges

Baking a cake can be very therapeutic. It lifts your spirits and produces
something good to eat. Don't worry if your cakes don't all turn out perfectly;
if you've used good ingredients, they will still taste good.

As well as an explanation of techniques and some useful tips, this chapter
contains recipes for some large-sized and small individual cakes; even though
they are fairly simple they will impress your family and friends. Whenever you
get the urge to bake something delicious but don't feel like making something
too complicated, this is the chapter to turn to time and time again.

CAKE-MAKING TECHNIQUES

Just alike any other aspect of cookery, cake-making comes with its own set of terms and techniques. The good news is that you only need to learn a few basic ones when you're just starting out – which is why the most common are explained here.

Creaming

Probably the most frequently used term in the cake-maker's vocabulary. It is the process of combining butter, sugar and air to produce a light-textured cake. Use only butter that is at room temperature. If creaming a mixture by hand, use either a wooden or silicone spoon to combine the butter and sugar. Beat the butter until soft, then add the sugar. Continue to beat the butter and sugar together until the mixture becomes lighter in colour and fluffy in texture. This can be done with a hand mixer to speed up the process, but don't overbeat; otherwise the air will start to escape.

Rubbing in

Rubbing in is a technique that is most commonly used when making shortbreads and some fruit loaves. Flour is sifted into the mixing bowl and butter is added in small pieces. The butter is then rubbed into the flour with the fingertips. Air is incorporated by raising the mixture as high as is sensible while the butter is being rubbed in. When the process is complete, the mixture should resemble breadcrumbs.

Folding in

This is the process of combining flour and a creamed mixture in a way that retains as much air in the cake as possible, which is what makes it light and such a joy to eat. Sifted flour is added gradually to creamed butter and sugar. Using a large metal spoon, cut into the mixture in one sweeping action, turning it over to combine but not beating. Mix the flour in this way until it has all been incorporated into the butter and sugar.

Dropping consistency

This is when a cake mixture is moist enough to fall readily off a spoon without any shaking. The mixture is then ready to bake.

Testing for doneness

To check if a cake is thoroughly baked, press the centre lightly with your index finger – it should feel springy and bounce back into shape. If not, bake for a few more minutes and repeat the test. This is the method I use, but you can also insert a toothpick into the centre of the cake if you prefer. If the toothpick comes out either clean or with just a few crumbs sticking to it, then the cake is done. If batter still clings to it, then return the cake to the oven for a few more minutes and test again.

Tips for successful cake-making
- Preheat the oven to the correct temperature.

- Read the recipe all the way through and prepare and weigh out all the ingredients before you begin.

- Prepare any tins or baking sheets before starting the recipe.

- Measure all ingredients accurately.

- Times given for cooking are approximate and will depend on your oven, so always bear this in mind when baking your cake.

- Once a cake is baked, transfer it to a cooling tray or wire rack; this allows air to circulate around it, cooling it more quickly and evenly.

Madeira Cake

One of the most versatile cake recipes, Madeira cake is simply a plain cake with a zesty flavour that can be spread with jam, lemon curd or your favourite preserve. Serve it with hot custard or cream and stewed fruit, or simply on its own with tea or coffee.

Makes 6–8 portions

180g butter
180g golden
   caster sugar
220g self-raising
   flour, sieved
4 small eggs, beaten
Zest of 1 lemon

1. Grease and line an 18cm round cake tin or 500g loaf tin. Preheat the oven to 170°C/gas mark 3.

2. Cream the butter and sugar until pale and fluffy.

3. Add 2 tablespoons of the flour, then gradually beat in the eggs.

4. Fold the rest of the flour into the mixture along with the lemon zest.

5. Spoon the mixture into the tin.

6. Bake for 45 minutes, then reduce the oven temperature to 150°C/gas mark 2 and bake for 45 minutes more. Test to see if it is done by pressing the centre lightly with your index finger – it should feel springy and bounce back into shape. If not, bake for a few more minutes and repeat the test.

7. Allow to cool for 10 minutes in the tin before removing and leave the paper on for 10 more minutes before removing.

8. When cool, store in an airtight tin. This will keep for at least 7 days.

Victoria Sandwich

A classic favourite. Although this recipe uses jam to sandwich the cake layers together, you could use any preserve or fruit filling instead. This cake will keep for five to six days in an airtight tin, but if you use fresh fruit for the filling, it won't keep as long.

Makes at least 10 large slices

200g butter, at
  room temperature
200g golden caster sugar
200g self-raising flour
3 eggs, beaten
2–3 tablespoons milk
Approximately 4
  tablespoons of
  your favourite jam,
  for filling

1. Grease 2 x 20cm round sandwich tins and line them with baking paper. Preheat the oven to 170°C/gas mark 3.

2. Cream the butter and sugar together in a mixing bowl until lighter in colour and fluffy in texture.

3. Add a tablespoon of the flour, then gradually beat in the eggs.

4. Fold in the rest of the flour using a metal tablespoon.

5. Stir in the milk, then divide the mixture evenly between the tins.

6. Level out the tops of each cake. Make a shallow well in the centre of each and bake for 18–20 minutes, or until risen and golden. Test to see if it is done by pressing the centre lightly with your index finger – it should feel springy and bounce back into shape. If not, bake for a few more minutes and repeat the test.

7. Remove from the oven and allow to cool for 15 minutes before lifting out of the tin. Cool for 5 more minutes on a wire rack before taking off the baking paper.

8. When the cakes are completely cool, spread the top of one of them with the jam (or other filling) and sandwich them together.

9. Place on a serving plate – I use an upturned tin lid lined with a paper doily; then you can cover the cake more easily with the tin. Dust a little caster sugar on the top before serving.

Fairy Cakes and Butterfly Buns

Use the Victoria Sandwich recipe on page 19 to make individual fairy cakes or butterfly buns – between 15–20 buns, depending upon how full the paper cases are. Fairy cakes are simply buns or cupcakes iced and decorated with chocolate chips, cherries, hundreds and thousands or any other cake decoration of your choice.

For the glacé icing
100g icing sugar
Sufficient water to
    mix to a thick but
    spreadable topping

For the buttercream
80g butter
120g icing sugar
¼ teaspoon
    vanilla extract

To make individual buns
1. Line 2 bun tins with paper cases. Preheat the oven to 170°C/ gas mark 3.

2. Prepare the cake mixture as in the Victoria Sandwich recipe on page 19 and spoon about a dessertspoon of the mixture into each bun case.

3. Bake for 12–15 minutes, until springy to the touch and golden brown.

4. Cool completely before decorating. These will keep for 4–5 days in an airtight tin.

For the glacé icing
1. Sieve the icing sugar into a bowl and mix with 2 tablespoons water to begin with. Add more water, a teaspoon at a time, until the icing is thick enough to stay on top of the cakes.

2. Decorate the tops and allow the icing to set before serving.

To make jam buns
Make the Victoria Sandwich cake mixture on page 19. Spoon the mixture into the paper cases as with Fairy Cakes, above, but before baking, drop half a teaspoon of your favourite jam into the centre of each bun. When they are cooked, the jam will drop to the bottom of the sponge. Cool completely, then dust them with icing sugar. These will keep for 5–6 days in an airtight tin.

To make butterfly buns
These buns contain vanilla-flavoured buttercream and will keep for 2–3 days in an airtight tin.

For the buttercream
1. Cream the butter until light and fluffy, sift in the icing sugar and vanilla, and beat until smooth and light.

2. Make the buns or cupcakes as before and allow to cool.

3. Cut a circle out of the centre of each cake and put a teaspoon of the buttercream in the space. Cut the top in half and put the pieces back in the centre of the buttercream to form 'butterfly wings'. Dust with icing sugar.

Golden Cake

This is an easy family cake with a syrupy taste. It can be eaten as a dessert with custard, or served as a teatime cake. It will keep for five to six days if stored in an airtight tin.

Make 10 portions

200g butter
180g golden caster sugar
200g self-raising flour
3 eggs
2 tablespoons
   golden syrup
½ teaspoon
   vanilla extract
3 tablespoons milk
A little caster sugar,
   for dusting

1. Preheat the oven to 170°C/gas mark 3. Grease and line the bottom of a 20cm loose-bottomed cake tin with baking paper.

2. Cream the butter and sugar together until light and fluffy.

3. Add a tablespoon of the flour and beat in the eggs gradually. Add the syrup and vanilla with the last lot of egg to be beaten in.

4. Fold in the flour and stir in the milk.

5. Spoon the mixture into the prepared tin and bake for 45–55 minutes, or until well risen and springy to the touch.

6. Allow to cool in the tin for 10 minutes before transferring to a cooling rack. Dust the top with caster sugar.

Variation
Add 100g sultanas to the mixture when you fold in the flour.

Low-fat Sponge Sandwich

This cake may not be fat-free, but it is lower in fat than a traditional sandwich cake – and it still has a good flavour.

Serves 6–8

For the sponge
80g softened butter
180g unrefined
   caster sugar
2 eggs
100g low-fat
   crème fraîche
200g self-raising flour

For the filling
80g icing sugar
1 tablespoon
   evaporated milk

1. Preheat the oven to 180°C/gas mark 4. Grease 2 x 20cm round sandwich tins and line them with baking parchment.

2. Cream the butter in a bowl until very light and fluffy, then cream in the sugar.

3. Beat the eggs into the crème fraîche.

4. Add half the flour to the creamed mixture. Add the egg mixture and beat well.

5. Fold the rest of the flour into the mixture and divide the mixture evenly between the tins.

6. Bake for 20–25 minutes, or until golden in colour and springy to the touch. Leave in the tin to cool for 10 minutes, then transfer to a cooling tray or wire rack.

7. To make the filling, sieve the icing sugar into a bowl and add the milk. Beat well; if it is too stiff, add another teaspoon of milk. If too runny, add a little more icing sugar.

8. When the cakes are cool, sandwich them together with the icing. Alternatively, sandwich them together with jam and use the icing as a topping.

Seed Cake

My grandma made this cake regularly. It it has a light yet creamy taste. It will keep for four to five days in an airtight tin.

Serves 8

150g butter
150g golden caster sugar
150g self-raising flour
3 eggs
50g ground almonds
2 teaspoons
  caraway seeds
4 tablespoons
  plain yoghurt

1. Preheat the oven to 180°C/gas mark 4. Grease and line a deep 18cm round cake tin.

2. Cream the butter and sugar together until light and soft.

3. Add a tablespoon of the flour and beat in the eggs gradually.

4. Sift the flour into the mixture and sprinkle in the almonds and seeds. Stir the dry ingredients into the mixture until thoroughly combined.

5. Stir in the yoghurt.

6. Spoon the mixture into the cake tin and bake for 50–55 minutes, or until well risen and golden in colour.

7. Cool in the tin for 10 minutes, then transfer to a cooling rack.

8. Sprinkle with a little extra caster sugar before serving.

Raspberry Jam Swiss Roll

A light cake that always goes down well with tea or coffee. This Swiss roll is filled with raspberry jam, but feel free to use any flavour – or lemon curd or marmalade. It is best eaten within 24 hours.

Serves 6–8

4 medium eggs
120g golden caster sugar
150g plain flour
25g ground almonds
5–6 tablespoons
   raspberry jam

1. Preheat the oven to 190°C/gas mark 5. Grease and line a 33cm x 23cm rectangular Swiss roll tin.

2. Whisk the eggs and sugar together until thick and pale.

3. Sieve the flour into the egg mixture and fold in lightly with a metal spoon.

4. Fold in the ground almonds.

5. Pour the mixture into the prepared tin and bake for 12–15 minutes. The sponge should be golden in colour and springy to the touch.

6. Leave to cool in the tin.

7. Lift the cake out of the tin and spread the surface with the jam. Roll up the sponge carefully, gently pulling away the baking parchment as you go. Sprinkle with a little extra caster sugar to serve.

Rich Genoese Sponge

This light yet rich cake can be cut in half and filled with jam, fruit purée or buttercream – or simply ice it on the top. It really tastes better if you can leave it for five to six hours before consuming, and will keep for three to four days in an airtight container.

Serves 8–10

4 eggs
120g golden caster sugar
120g plain flour sieved
    with a pinch salt
    and ½ teaspoon
    baking powder
50g butter, softened
    to become runny
    but not separated

1. Preheat the oven to 190°C/gas mark 5.

2. Lightly grease a 20cm round cake tin and place a disc of baking paper in the bottom. Grease the paper lightly. Dust the whole tin with a little caster sugar, then flour. Make sure you get rid of the excess in both cases.

3. Place a large, heatproof mixing bowl over a pan of barely simmering water. Put the eggs and sugar into the mixing bowl and whisk with either a balloon whisk or an electric whisk until the mixture has doubled in size and leaves thick ribbons of mixture on the sides of the bowl. Remove from the heat and cool for a few minutes, whisking gently occasionally.

4. Sieve the flour again, this time into the egg and sugar mixture, and fold it in.

5. Drizzle the melted butter around the edges of the bowl in thin ribbons, then fold in gently.

6. Pour the mixture into the prepared tin and bake for 20–30 minutes. The cake should be well risen and springy to the touch, and it will be wrinkled around the edges.

7. Cool in the tin for 10 minutes, then transfer to a cooling rack. Remove the paper. Cool completely before slicing in half and filling.

8. Decorate with glacé icing or buttercream (see page 8) if desired.

Fresh Cream Sponge

A real treat for cream-lovers. You can buy these cakes quite cheaply in the shops, but they don't taste as good as this one! It will also keep for up to three days in a container in the fridge.

Serves 6–8

110g self-raising flour
30g cornflour
120g butter
120g golden caster sugar
2 eggs plus 1 egg yolk,
    beaten together
120ml double cream
4 tablespoons
    strawberry jam

1. Preheat the oven to 180°C/gas mark 4. Grease and line 2 x 20cm sandwich tins.

2. Sieve the 2 flours together into a small bowl or dish.

3. Cream the butter and sugar until light and fluffy. Add 1 tablespoons of the flour and beat in the eggs gradually. Fold in the flour.

4. Divide the mixture between the tins and bake for 15 minutes, or until they are well risen and springy.

5. Cool for 10 minutes in the tin, then transfer to a wire rack to cool completely.

6. Whisk the cream until light yet thickened sufficiently not to run out of the cake.

7. Spread the top of one cake layer with the jam, then add the cream. Sandwich the layers together and dust the top of the cake with a little caster sugar.

Iced Topped Ginger Sponge

Ginger-lovers will adore this. It contains three varieties of ginger: ground, stem in syrup and crystallised. If you wish, leave the cake un-iced and serve it with custard or cream as a dessert.

Serves 8–10

150g butter
120g soft
   dark-brown sugar
3 tablespoons
   golden syrup
200g self-raising flour
1 teaspoon
   ground ginger
½ teaspoon
   ground cinnamon
3 eggs, beaten
4 tablespoons milk
3–4 pieces of stem
   ginger in syrup,
   chopped

For the glacé icing
80g icing sugar
A few drops of
   water to mix

4–5 pieces
   crystallised ginger

1. Preheat the oven to 170°C/gas mark 3. Grease and line the bottom of a 22cm round tin.

2. Cream the butter, sugar and syrup together until the mixture is fluffy and lighter in colour.

3. Sieve the flour and spices together into a separate bowl. Add 1 tablespoon of the flour mixture to the creamed mixture, then beat in the eggs and milk.

4. Add the flour gradually and fold in. As you do so, add the stem ginger.

5. Spoon the mixture into the prepared tin and bake for 40–45 minutes, or until the cake is well risen and springy.

6. Cool in the tin for 10 minutes before transferring to a cooling rack.

7. Make the glacé icing by mixing the sugar and water into a thick yet spreadable mixture and smooth over the top of the cooled cake.

8. Decorate with the crystallised ginger pieces.

Carrot Cake

It comes as a great surprise to many that carrots are sweet, but when they taste carrot cake they are convinced. A good carrot cake is moist, sweet and as good on its own as it is topped with buttercream or icing.

Serves 8–10

200ml sunflower or
  vegetable oil
200g golden caster sugar
3 eggs, beaten
350g grated carrots
3 tablespoons raisins
  or sultanas
150g self-raising flour
150g self-raising
  wholemeal flour
2 tablespoons fresh
  orange juice
2 level teaspoons
  mixed spice

For the cream-cheese
  frosting
120g light soft
  cream cheese
30g half-fat crème fraîche
100g icing sugar

1. Preheat the oven to 180°C/gas mark 4. Grease and line a 20cm square tin.

2. Whisk the oil, sugar and eggs together in a mixing bowl until light and creamy.

3. Stir in the carrots and the fruit.

4. Sieve the flours and mixed spice together into a separate bowl, but stir in any bits of wholemeal flour that may remain in the sieve.

5. Fold the combined flours into the egg mixture, then stir in the orange juice.

6. Pour into the prepared tin and bake for 40–50 minutes. Push a skewer into the centre to see if it is done; if there is still mixture on the skewer, then bake for 5 more minutes and test again.

7. Leave to cool in the tin for 10 minutes, then transfer to a cooling tray.

8. While the cake cools completely, make the cream cheese frosting by putting the three ingredients into a mixing bowl and whisking together until light and smooth.

9. Spread the frosting over the carrot cake and cut it into squares. Sprinkle with a little grated orange zest on top to serve.

Coconut Cake

I love coconut in all its forms, but this is my favourite way of eating it. It will keep for four to five days in an airtight tin, although it is best eaten within three days.

Serves 8

150g butter
150g caster sugar
150g self-raising
   flour, sifted
3 eggs, beaten
2 tablespoons powdered
   coconut milk mixed
   with 4 tablespoons
   warm water to make
   a smooth cream
50g desiccated coconut
3 tablespoons seedless
   raspberry jam
1 tablespoon desiccated
   coconut, for topping

1. Preheat the oven to 170°C/gas mark 3. Grease and line an 18cm round cake tin.

2. Cream the butter and sugar together until light and fluffy.

3. Add 1 tablespoon of the flour and beat in the eggs.

4. Add another tablespoon of flour and beat in the coconut cream.

5. Sieve the rest of the flour into the creamed mixture and fold in, adding the desiccated coconut as you do so.

6. Spoon the mixture into the prepared tin and bake for 35–40 minutes, or until the cake is well risen, golden in colour and springy to the touch.

7. Allow to cool for 10 minutes in the tin, then take out of the tin and transfer to a cooling rack. Allow to cool for a further 15–20 minutes before removing the paper.

8. Spread the jam over the top of the cake and sprinkle with the coconut.

Variation
Toast the coconut for the topping for added colour and flavour: heat the grill to its hottest setting, put the coconut on a small baking sheet and toast until golden brown. Watch it at all times – this only takes a few seconds.

Coffee Sandwich Cake

Coffee-lovers take note: the sponge, icing and buttercream filling are all flavoured with your favourite beverage. Using granulated sugar for this recipe results in a cake with gives it a denser texture that holds the buttercream and icing better. Mix the coffee with the hot water before starting to make the cake so that it will be cold when you add it to the creamed mixture. The coffee listed in the cake ingredients is used for the cake, buttercream and fudge icing.

Serves 8

For the cake
150g butter
150g golden
    granulated sugar
150g self-raising flour
3 eggs, beaten
1 rounded dessertspoon
    coffee granules mixed
    with 3 dessertspoons
    hot water

For the buttercream
80g butter
150g sieved icing sugar
Half of the rest of the
    coffee mixture, above

For the fudge icing
50g butter
50g soft brown sugar
The rest of the coffee
    mixture, above
180g icing sugar, sieved
1 tablespoon evaporated
    milk
1 dessertspoon
    golden syrup

For decoration
Chocolate-coated
    coffee beans

To make the cake
1. Preheat the oven to 170°C/gas mark 3. Grease and line the bottom of 2 x 20cm sandwich tins.

2. Cream the butter and sugar together until light and fluffy. Add 1 tablespoon of the flour and half the eggs and beat well.

3. Add the rest of the eggs and half the coffee mixture. Beat again.

4. Sift the flour into the creamed mixture and fold in.

5. Divide the mixture between the tins and bake for 15–20 minutes, or until springy to the touch.

6. Allow to cool for 10 minutes in the tins, then transfer the cakes to a cooling rack. Remove the paper when cool.

To make the buttercream
1. Beat the butter until soft.

2. Add the icing sugar and the coffee mixture and beat together until creamy and light. Use to sandwich the two halves of the cake together.

To make the fudge icing
1. Melt the butter, brown sugar and golden syrup together in a pan over a very low heat and stir until the sugar dissolves.

2. Add the coffee mixture and half of the icing sugar and the evaporated milk. Remove from the heat and beat everything well.

3. Add the rest of the icing sugar and beat well again. Continue beating until the icing is thick and smooth.

4. Spread over the top of the cake in a thick layer. Decorate with chocolate-coated coffee beans, if desired.

Yorkshire Parkin

A very tasty and easy cake to make, especially in the autumnal months. Parkin develops a stickiness if left for 24 hours before eating; the flavour is better, too, so make it the day before you want to eat it.

Serves 8

1 level teaspoon
   ground ginger
130g self-raising flour
130g fine oatmeal
50g butter
2 tablespoons
   black treacle
2 tablespoons
   golden syrup
50g brown sugar
1 egg
2 tablespoons milk

1. Preheat the oven to 170°C/gas mark 3. Grease a 15cm square tin.

2. Sieve the ginger with the flour into a large mixing bowl and stir in the oatmeal.

3. Melt the butter with the treacle, syrup and sugar together in a pan over a very low heat. As soon as the butter has melted, remove from the heat, stir well and beat in the egg.

4. Pour the buttery mixture into the flour and mix vigorously with a wooden spoon.

5. Add the milk and beat again; it should be a soft, pourable mixture. If not, add another tablespoon milk.

6. Pour the mixture into the tin and bake for 50–55 minutes; it should be firm to the touch in the centre when cooked. If not, bake for 5 more minutes.

7. Allow to cool in the tin on a cooling rack. After 10 minutes, cut into 12 equal squares.

8. When completely cool, lift the squares out of the tin and transfer to an airtight tin.

Variation
If you love raisins, add 50g to the mixture at step 5 when adding the milk and stir in well.

Honey Cake

Honey has been a sweetening ingredient for centuries. Even when sugar was available it cost more than the average household could afford, so honey was used instead. In this recipe it helps to make a moist cake that stays fresh longer than most cakes made with sugar. This will keep in an airtight container for at least five to six days.

Serves 8–10

150ml clear honey
250g wholemeal flour
3 eggs, beaten
100g ground almonds
½ teaspoon mixed spice
½ teaspoon
  ground cinnamon
2 teaspoons
  baking powder
3 tablespoons milk
10–12 halved almonds

1. Preheat the oven to 170°C/gas mark 3. Grease a 20cm round cake tin and line it with baking paper.

2. Warm the honey in a heatproof glass bowl set in a pan of very hot water. When it is warm, remove from the water and whisk until the honey is thick and frothy.

3. Add a tablespoon of flour, sprinkling it over the surface of the honey.

4. Whisk in the eggs gradually.

5. Stir the ground almonds and spices into the rest of the flour and add it gradually to the honey mixture.

6. Stir the baking powder into the milk, then beat this into the cake mixture.

7. Spoon the mixture into the cake tin and press the almonds into the top.

8. Bake for 25–30 minutes until well risen, but don't leave in too long or the honey will overcook and begin to taste bitter.

9. Allow the cake to cool completely in the tin, then transfer it to a cooling rack.

Battenberg

This sponge cake is trickier to make than any other in this chapter, but it tastes better than any shop-bought version. It is a marzipan-lover's heaven, and you can have as thick a layer of marzipan as the quantity will allow. Battenberg cake is traditionally half yellow and half pink, but here I've done away with artificial colourings and made it with coffee here so that one half is plain and the other is light brown. It is delicious made with the homemade marzipan on the next page, but if you prefer, it can be finished with ready-made.

Serves 6

150g butter
150g caster sugar
2 eggs, beaten
150g self-raising flour
2 tablespoons milk
1 level teaspoon coffee
  mixed with 3
  teaspoons of
  boiling water
1 quantity of marzipan
  (see next page); if
  buying ready-made,
  use 2 x 250g packs

Apricot jam, for
  assembling the cake

1. Preheat the oven to 170°C/gas mark 3. Grease and line 2 x 20cm tins with baking paper.

2. Cream the butter and sugar together. Beat in the eggs.

3. Sieve the flour into the creamed mixture and fold it in along with the milk.

4. Put half of the mixture into 1 of the tins and smooth it out; it won't come very high up the tin, but don't worry – this is OK.

5. Add the coffee to the remaining mixture and stir in well. Spoon this into the second tin and smooth out as before. The colour of the mixtures will look very similar at this stage, but they will look quite different once they are baked.

6. Bake for 20–25 minutes, then allow to cool for 10 minutes before removing from the tins and transferring to a cooling rack.

To assemble the cake
1. Trim the coffee sponge to make as perfect a rectangle as you can. You can eat the trimmings, make them into a small queen of puddings or use as a trifle base.

2. Do the same with the plain sponge.

3. Cut each cake lengthways into 2 equal strips.

4. Sandwich each plain strip to a coffee strip with apricot jam, then spread apricot jam over the top face of one assembled cake and sandwich the other to it so that you have a coffee section on top of plain and a plain section on top of coffee. *(continued on next page)*
To make the marzipan

Battenberg *(continued)*

For the marzipan
175g icing sugar
175g caster sugar
350g ground almonds
2 teaspoon lemon juice
¼–½ teaspoon
   almond extract
1 whole egg plus an
   extra white,
   beaten together

1. Sieve the two sugars together into a mixing bowl and stir in the almonds.

2. Add the lemon juice and almond extract. The first time you make this, try using just ¼ teaspoon of almond extract as some brands have a stronger flavour than others; you can always add more the next time.

3. Add half of the egg mixture and stir in.

4. Use your hands to knead the mixture, adding more egg until it becomes a soft, pliable dough. Knead the marzipan for 1 minute.

5. Dust a work surface with icing sugar. Roll out the marzipan until it is about 5mm deep (or to your preference) and is large enough to fit all round the cake.

6. Brush the entire surface of the marzipan with a little apricot jam and lay the cake carefully in the centre.

7. Wrap the marzipan around the cake and press gently down to secure the ends; brush any overlap with a little jam to stick it down. Leave uncovered for about 2 hours to dry out the marzipan a little, then store in an airtight tin for 2–3 days.

SIMPLE CAKES AND SPONGES
My Notes

3
Fruit and Nut Cakes

This chapter has been designed for lovers of all types of fruit and nut cakes, using dried and fresh fruit and all kinds of nuts. Some recipes are rich and rather extravagant for special occasions while others are simple, everyday cakes. All, however, are delicious.

Currant Buns

Easy and delicious, these are a treat with afternoon tea.

Makes 12 good-sized buns

130g butter
130g golden caster sugar
150g self-raising flour
2 eggs, beaten
50–60g currants
3 tablespoons milk

1. Preheat the oven to 170°C/gas mark 3. Place 12 bun cases in a 12-hole bun tin. If you wish to make larger ones, use muffin paper cases.

2. Cream the butter and sugar together until light and fluffy.

3. Sieve in 1 tablespoon of the flour, then add the eggs and beat in well.

4. Sift in the rest of the flour and fold it into the creamed mixture, adding the currants and folding them in along with the flour.

5. Stir in the milk to make a soft dropping consistency; add more milk if necessary.

6. Spoon about a dessertspoonful into each paper case; too much and the mixture will spill over the side.

7. Bake for 12–15 minutes, or until well risen and springy to the touch.

Rock Buns

These are so easy to make and are very versatile. You can also vary the ingredients easily.

Makes 12–15

100g butter, cut into
 small cubes
200g self-raising flour
100g soft brown sugar
25g glacé cherries,
 chopped
25g sultanas
4 tablespoons milk
1 egg

1. Preheat the oven to 180°C/gas mark 4. Grease 2 baking sheets.

2. Rub the butter into the flour until the mixture looks like breadcrumbs. Stir in the sugar and fruit.

3. Whisk the milk into the egg and stir into the cake mixture.

4. Combine well and spoon rough rounds of the mixture onto the baking sheets – about 2cm apart.

5. Bake for about 20 minutes, or until golden and firm to the touch.

Variations
Try the following in place of the cherries and/or sultanas:

• 30g chocolate chips

• 25g chopped walnuts and 25g of chopped dates

• 30g fresh blueberries

• 1 tablespoon orange marmalade and 25g chopped mixed peel

• ½ teaspoon cinnamon and a peeled, chopped apple

Dundee Cake

This is a real family favourite. Because it is a rich recipe, it will keep well, too, and tastes best if allowed to mature for three days before eating. It will keep for at least three weeks, so long as it is well wrapped up and kept in the airtight container.

Makes 10–12 generous portions

200g butter
200g soft brown sugar
250g plain flour, sifted
5 eggs
200g sultanas
125g currants
30g ground almonds
80g glacé cherries,
    rinsed of the syrup
    and dried well
50g mixed chopped
    peel, optional
Juice and zest of
    1 lemon
Juice and zest of
    half an orange
30g whole almonds

1. Preheat the oven to 150°C/gas mark 2. Grease and line a 23cm round cake tin.

2. Cream the butter and the sugar together until light and fluffy.

3. Add a tablespoon of the flour and gradually beat in the eggs.

4. Put all the dried fruit together in a bowl and sprinkle with 2 tablespoons flour and the ground almonds. Mix well with a large spoon.

5. Fold in the flour and stir in the fruit mixture. Add the juice and zests of the fruit and stir in.

6. Spoon the mixture into the tin and press down lightly to make sure the mixture has no air bubbles in the base. Smooth out the top and make a shallow dip in the centre to allow for a hilly centre to the finished cake.

7. Arrange the almonds on the top in concentric circles.

8. Bake for 1½–2 hours, but check the cake after 40 minutes: if it is beginning to brown too quickly, cover with a piece of foil (make sure it doesn't actually touch the cake, though).

9. After 1½ hours, test the centre of the cake with a metal skewer; if it comes out clean, the cake is done. If there is any mixture still clinging to the skewer, however, then it needs extra baking time.

10. When the cake is done, place it, still in the tin, on a cooling rack for 15 minutes. Lift out of the tin and cool for 20 minutes before removing the paper.

11. Allow to cool completely before wrapping in greaseproof paper and foil and storing in an airtight container.

Moist Cherry Cake

Remember to serve this rich cake in small slices as it is very filling.

Serves 10–12

200g butter
180g golden caster sugar
½ teaspoon almond extract (more expensive than essence but it has a much better flavour)
70g self-raising flour
6 eggs, beaten
180g ground almonds
250g glacé cherries

1. Preheat the oven to 170°C/gas mark 3. Grease and line a 23cm round loose-bottomed tin with baking paper.

2. Cream the butter and sugar together and stir in the almond extract.

3. Add a tablespoon of the flour and beat in the eggs. Add more flour if necessary.

4. Add the rest of the flour and stir it in along with the almonds.

5. Arrange the cherries in the tin and pour the cake mixture on top.

6. Bake for 45–50 minutes until the cake is firm to the touch.

7. Leave to cool in the tin. Remove and take off the paper, then dust with icing sugar before serving.

Easy Simmered Fruit Cake

If you love a rich fruit cake but want easy preparation, then this is the recipe to choose. Try adding a tablespoon of Jack Daniels with the fruit in step 1 for an extra-special taste.

Serves 10–12

200g mixed dried fruit
200g soft brown sugar
200ml milk
200g butter
1 tablespoon honey
1 level teaspoon
   mixed spice
280 self-raising flour
2 eggs, beaten

1. Preheat the oven to 150°C/gas mark 2. Grease and line a 20cm round cake tin.

2. Put the fruit, sugar, milk, butter, honey and spice in a pan on a medium heat. Bring to a gentle simmer and continue to simmer for 5 minutes.

3. Take off heat and allow to cool completely before sieving in half of the flour and beating in the eggs.

4. Add the rest of the flour and fold it into cake mixture until fully combined.

5. Spoon the mixture into the cake tin and smooth out the top, making a well in the centre to allow for when the cake rises.

6. Bake for 40 minutes at 150°C/gas mark 2, then turn oven down to 140°C/gas mark 1 for 20–30 minutes, or until firm to the touch and dark golden-brown in colour. Test the centre of the cake with a skewer or thin knife; if it is ready, there should be no cake mixture on the blade. If it requires further baking time, cover it with foil and leave to bake for a further 10–15 minutes.

7. Leave the cake in the tin to cool for 30–40 minutes, then remove it and peel away the paper. Leave to cool completely on a wire rack before wrapping in greaseproof paper and placing in an airtight container. Allow the flavour and moistness to develop for 1–2 days before eating.

Village Bara Brith

This is a very easy version of traditional Welsh *bara brith*, or 'currant bread'. It is very economical and tastes better if you allow it to mature for a day before slicing, and it is wonderful sliced and spread with butter.

Serves 8–10

280g dried mixed fruit
150g soft brown sugar
450ml cold tea
350g self-raising flour
1 teaspoon mixed spice
1 teaspoon baking
   powder
2 eggs, beaten

1. Put the fruit and sugar together in a large mixing bowl. Combine well with a wooden spoon, then add the cold tea. Leave to soak overnight.

2. Preheat the oven to 150°C/gas mark 2. Butter a 1kg loaf tin.

3. Sift the flour, spice and baking powder together into the fruit mixture and stir well. Beat in the eggs.

4. Pour the mixture into the prepared loaf tin and bake for 1½ hours.

5. Allow to cool in the tin for 15 minutes, then transfer to a wire rack.

6. When completely cool, wrap in greaseproof paper and store in an airtight tin.

Coffee and Walnut Cake

Use pecans in place of walnuts for a change, if you prefer.

Serves 8

150g butter
150g soft brown sugar
2 teaspoons good
  granulated coffee
  mixed with a
  tablespoon of
  hot water
150g self-raising flour
2 eggs, beaten
50g chopped walnuts
2–3 tablespoons milk
Whole walnuts,
  to decorate

*For the coffee
  buttercream*
75g butter
100g icing sugar
1 teaspoon granulated
  coffee mixed with 2
  teaspoons hot water

1. Preheat the oven to 170°C/gas mark 3. Grease and line a 20cm round loose-bottomed tin with baking or greaseproof paper.

2. Cream the butter and sugar together until light and fluffy. Beat in the coffee.

3. Add a tablespoon of the flour and beat in the eggs.

4. Fold in the flour and add the walnuts as you do so.

5. Stir in sufficient milk to make a dropping consistency.

6. Spoon the mixture into the prepared tin and bake for about 35 minutes, or until well risen and springy to the touch.

7. Allow to cool for 15 minutes in the tin, then transfer to a wire rack to cool completely. Leave for a few minutes before removing the paper.

8. While the cake cools, make the buttercream. Beat the butter until soft and cream in the icing sugar and coffee. When the mixture is light and fluffy it is ready to use.

9. Make sure the cake is completely cold before topping with the buttercream or it will melt. Decorate the finished cake with some whole walnuts if you wish.

Farmhouse Fruit Cake

A lightly spiced, sugar-topped fruit cake.

Serves 8–10

180g butter
180g golden caster sugar
220g self-raising flour
2 medium eggs
½ level teaspoon
  cinnamon
A pinch nutmeg
Zest of 1 lemon
25g currants
50g raisins
25g sultanas
4 tablespoons milk
1 dessertspoon
  demerara sugar,
  for topping

1. Preheat the oven to 180°C/gas mark 4. Grease and line an 18cm round tin.

2. Cream the butter and sugar together until very light and fluffy.

3. Add a tablespoon of the flour and beat in the eggs.

4. Sieve the flour and spices together into the creamed mixture and begin to fold in.

5. Add the lemon zest and dried fruit and fold in.

6. Stir in the milk, then spoon the mixture into the prepared tin. Sprinkle the dessertspoon of demerara sugar over the top at this stage for a crispy topping.

7. Bake for 1–1¼ hours, or until deep golden in colour.

8. Allow to cool in the tin for 10 minutes, then remove the cake from the tin and allow it to cool completely on a cooling rack before slicing.

Cherry and Sultana Ring Cake

This cake may have an unusual preparation, but the result is light and airy and not too sweet. It is an ideal after-dinner cake to serve with coffee and will keep for about three days.

Serves 10–12

100g plain flour, sifted
100g butter
100g sultanas
50g glacé cherries, washed, dried well and halved
Grated zest of 1 lemon
4 eggs, separated
100g golden caster sugar
2 teaspoons icing sugar, for dusting

1. Preheat the oven to 220°C/gas mark 7. Grease and lightly flour a 20cm ring cake tin.

2. Sift the flour again into a mixing bowl.

3. Cut the butter into small pieces and stir into the flour. Lightly rub it in with your fingertips.

4. Stir in the sultanas, cherries and lemon zest. Make sure everything is well-coated in the flour.

5. Whisk the egg whites until they are light and fluffy and form firm peaks. Beat half of the sugar into the egg whites. The mixture should be glossy.

6. Beat the rest of the sugar into the egg yolks and fold this into the whisked whites.

7. Add a third of the flour mixture to the eggs and fold in; do this with another third and finally the last third. Take great care to fold and don t be tempted to mix it in. It won't necessarily look totally combined, but this will happen as it bakes.

8. Pour the mixture into the prepared tin and level it out with the back of a metal spoon.

9. Bake for 15 minutes, then reduce the temperature to 180°C/gas mark 4 and bake for 25–30 minutes more, or until it has turned a deep golden brown.

10. Cool in the tin for 5 minutes, then turn out onto a cooling rack.

11. Allow to cool for 15 minutes more, then dust with icing sugar. When completely cool, store in an airtight tin.

Cherry and Marzipan Cake

Marzipan bakes inside this cake – which makes a delicious surprise when you eat it. Stored in an airtight tin, it will keep for four to five days.

Serves 6–8

220g butter
200g golden caster sugar
220g self-raising flour
3 eggs, beaten
50g ground almonds
2 tablespoons milk
150g marzipan (see page 11), diced into 5mm cubes
100g glacé cherries, rinsed and dried

1. Preheat the oven to 170°C/gas mark 3. Grease and line a 20cm loose-bottomed cake tin.

2. Cream the butter and sugar together until pale and fluffy. Add 1 tablespoon of the flour and beat in the eggs gradually.

3. Sift the flour into the creamed mixture and fold it in, adding the ground almonds as you do so. Stir in the milk.

4. Fold in the cherries and marzipan gently until evenly mixed in.

5. Spoon the mixture into the prepared tin and bake for 50–60 minutes. Test with a skewer to see if the cake is baked in the centre.

6. Allow to cool for 10 minutes before removing the cake from the tin. Transfer it to a wire rack and remove the paper after about 10 more minutes.

Pear Upside-down Cake

This is often made with pineapples and was one of the first cakes I made when my husband and I got married. This spicy version lends itself to autumn and winter months and will keep for three to four days.

Serves 8

2 tablespoons
   clear honey
2 tablespoons soft
   brown sugar
2 large pears, peeled,
   cored and sliced into
   about 8 slices each
120g butter
100g golden caster sugar
140g self-raising flour
2 eggs, beaten
1 teaspoon mixed spice
2 tablespoons milk

1. Preheat the oven to 180°C/gas mark 4. Grease and line a 20cm loose-bottomed cake tin.

2. Put the honey and brown sugar in a small pan and place over a very low heat. Stir until the honey is very runny and the sugar has combined evenly with it.

3. Pour into the prepared tin and swirl it around so that the base of the tin is covered with the honey mixture.

4. Arrange the pears in the honey mixture in concentric circles.

5. Beat the butter and caster sugar together until pale and fluffy. Add a tablespoon of the flour and beat in the eggs.

6. Sift in the flour and mixed spice at the same time and fold into the creamed mixture. Stir in the milk gently.

7. Carefully spoon the cake mixture onto the pears and smooth out the top.

8. Bake for 45–50 minutes, or until well risen, golden brown and springy in the centre.

9. Allow to cool for 20 minutes in the tin, then transfer the cake to a cooling rack. Cool for another 20 minutes before removing the paper. Store in an airtight tin.

Pecan and Prune Cake

This is a rich, slightly chocolatey cake. The prunes make it moist and give it a good depth of flavour, and it will keep for five to six days when stored in an airtight tin.

Serves 10–12

220g butter
220g soft brown sugar
220g self-raising flour
5 eggs
25g cocoa powder
400g ready-to-eat
   prunes, chopped
180g pecans, chopped
50g chocolate chips
   (plain or milk)

1. Preheat the oven to 180°C/gas mark 4. Grease and line a 20cm square tin with baking paper.

2. Cream the butter and sugar together until it is soft and fluffy.

3. Sift in 2 tablespoons of the flour and start to beat in the eggs gradually. Add another tablespoon of flour halfway through beating in the eggs.

4. Sift the rest of the flour and cocoa together into the creamed mixture and fold in.

5. Stir in the rest of the ingredients.

6. Spoon the mixture into the tin and wrap 2 layers of brown paper around the outside of it. Secure with string. Place a sheet of brown paper on a baking tray and stand the cake on it.

7. Bake for 1½–1¾ hours, or until done in the centre. Test with a skewer; it should come out clean and free from cake mixture.

8. Cool in the tin for 20–30 minutes, then place on a wire rack to cool completely.

Cherry Genoa Cake

This cake is made with a small amount of flour and ground almonds. Adding cornflour gives it a very light, melt-in-the-mouth texture, and it will keep for four to five days.

Serves 8

150g butter
150g golden caster sugar
100g ground almonds
3 eggs
30g cornflour
50g self-raising flour
50g glacé cherries,
    washed, dried
    and halved

1. Preheat the oven to 180°C/gas mark 4. Grease a 18cm round tin and line it with baking paper.

2. Cream the butter and sugar together until pale and fluffy. Cream in the almonds.

3. Beat in the eggs gradually, adding a little flour if necessary.

4. Sift the two flours together first into a bowl, then again into the creamed mixture and fold in.

5. Stir in the cherries, and spoon the mixture into the tin.

6. Bake for 35–45 minutes, or until well risen and a deep golden brown.

7. Allow to cool in the tin for 20 minutes before transferring to a wire rack. Store in in an airtight tin.

Apple Sauce Cake

The wonderful flavours of apples, cinnamon and nutmeg take some beating, and this cake contains all three. You can store it for three to four days in an airtight tin – if it lasts that long!

Makes 10 portions

130g butter
130g brown sugar
80g stewed Bramley
  apples, puréed
180g self-raising flour
½ level teaspoon
  ground cinnamon
½ level teaspoon
  ground nutmeg
80g raisins

1. Preheat the oven to 150°C/gas mark 2. Grease and line an 18cm round tin.

2. Cream the butter and sugar together until fluffy and stir in the apples.

3. Sift in the flour with the spices and fold in with a wooden spoon. If the mixture is too stiff, add a tablespoon of milk.

4. Stir in the raisins.

5. Spoon the mixture into the prepared tin and bake for 1 hour.

6. Allow the cake to cool in the tin for 10 minutes before transferring to a wire rack.

Danish Apple Cake

This more of a dessert than a cake, but it can be served cold with tea or coffee.

Makes 8 portions

150g butter
150g golden caster sugar
150g self-raising flour
2 eggs
25g ground almonds
30g sultanas
3 dessert apples, peeled,
  cored and sliced
2 tablespoons soft
  brown sugar mixed
  with 2 level teaspoons
  ground cinnamon
20g flaked almonds

1. Preheat the oven to 180°C/gas mark 4. Butter a 20cm cake tin.

2. Cream the butter and sugar together in a mixing bowl.

3. Add 1 tablespoon of flour and beat in the eggs. Fold in the flour and ground almonds and stir in the sultanas.

4. Put half of the cake mixture in the tin and smooth out the top. Put a layer of the apples over the top and sprinkle with half of the sugar and cinnamon mixture.

5. Spoon the rest of the cake mixture over the apples. Top with the rest of the apples and sprinkle with the sugar and cinnamon mixture.

6. Spread the flaked almonds evenly over the top.

7. Bake for 40–45 minutes until the cake is firm yet springy to the touch.

8. Leave to cool in the tin for 10 minutes before transferring to a serving plate if you're serving it hot. If not, transfer to a wire rack. Store in an airtight tin.

Pineapple and Mixed Fruit Cake

This recipe uses unusual dried fruits that are now readily available on the supermarket shelves. It makes a great alternative to traditional Christmas cake for those who prefer a lighter taste.

Serves 8–10

50g each of dried pineapple, raisins and cherries
25g chopped ready-to-eat apricots
150ml pineapple juice
150g self-raising flour
1 teaspoon ground cinnamon
100g wholemeal flour
A little grated nutmeg
220g butter
180g soft brown sugar
3 eggs beaten

1. Preheat the oven to 170°C/gas mark 3. Grease and line an 18cm deep cake tin.

2. Put the dried fruit into a bowl and pour in the pineapple juice. Stir well and leave for 1 hour before starting to mix the cake.

3. Sift the self-raising flour and cinnamon into a mixing bowl. Stir in the wholemeal flour and nutmeg.

4. Rub the butter into the flour until the mixture resembles breadcrumbs.

5. Stir in the sugar until well mixed. Beat in the eggs.

6. Spoon the mixture into the tin and smooth out the top, making a well in the centre.

7. Bake for 35–40 minutes until well risen and test the centre of the cake with a skewer to see if it is baked. If not, bake for another 5–10 minutes, then test again.

8. Allow it to cool in the tin for 10 minutes, then transfer to a wire rack. Remove the paper carefully. This will keep for 10–15 days if wrapped in greaseproof paper and stored in an airtight tin.

Orange Polenta Cake

Polenta gives this cake an interesting texture, and the orange syrup marries very well with the cake. This may be served as a cake or with thin slices of fresh orange and some crème fraîche as a dessert.

Serves 8–10

175g butter
175g golden caster sugar
150g ground almonds
2 large eggs
½ teaspoon baking
  powder
100g polenta
Zest and juice of
  1 orange

For the syrup
3 tablespoons honey
Zest and juice of
  2 oranges
1 tablespoon brandy or
  Cointreau, optional

1. Preheat the oven to 180°C/gas mark 4. Grease and line a 20cm square cake tin with baking paper.

2. Cream the butter and sugar together in a mixing bowl until light and fluffy.

3. Stir in the almonds and beat in the eggs.

4. Add the baking powder to the polenta and combine well.

5. Mix the polenta into the creamed mixture along with the orange juice and zest.

6. Spoon the mixture into the prepared tin and bake for 20 minutes, then turn down the heat to 170°C/gas mark 3 and bake for a further 35–40 minutes until the cake is firm.

7. Leave the cake in the tin while you make the syrup. In a small pan on a very low heat, stir the honey into the juice and zest of the orange and add the brandy.

8. Prick the cake all over with a skewer and pour the warm juice evenly over the entire cake. Leave to cool for 30 minutes, then remove from the tin and allow to cool completely before removing the paper.

Rich Tea Loaf

This moist, rich fruit cake uses no fat in its preparation – except for what you use to grease the tin.

Makes 10–12 portions

120g sultanas
120g raisins
100g currants
120g glacé cherries
180g dark brown sugar
300ml cold tea,
   normal strength
300g self-raising flour
1 egg

1. Put the dried fruit and sugar in a bowl and pour in the cold tea. Mix well and leave to soak overnight.

2. Preheat the oven to 180°C/gas mark 4. Grease a 1kg loaf tin and line it with baking paper.

3. Sieve the flour into the tea and fruit mixture and add the egg. Beat everything well together.

4. Pour the mixture into the prepared tin.

5. Bake for 1¼–1½ hours and test the centre with a skewer to see if it is done.

6. For an extra-special finish: while the cake is still in the tin and very hot, prick it with a skewer all over and drizzle 3 tablespoons brandy or whisky over the surface. Leave for 10 minutes, then remove from the tin.

7. Allow to cool for 10 more minutes and remove the paper. Transfer to a wire rack and cool completely. This will keep in an airtight tin for 6–7 days.

Lemon Drizzle Loaf

A real lemony cake that makes a refreshing change from a Madeira cake. It will keep for four to five days in an airtight container.

Serves 8–10

150g butter
150g golden caster sugar
170g self-raising flour
25g dried candied lemon peel, chopped
2 eggs, beaten
Juice and zest of 1 lemon

For the icing
60g icing sugar
1–2 tablespoons lemon juice
Very thin strips of lemon zest (not the pith), sufficient to decorate the top of the cake.

1. Preheat the oven to 180°C/gas mark 4. Grease and line a 23cm loaf tin with baking paper.

2. Put all the cake ingredients except the lemon zest into a large mixing bowl and whisk together with a hand mixer. Start on the slowest speed then build up to the fastest as the ingredients begin to blend. Whisk for about 5 minutes until the mixture is lighter in colour.

3. Stir in the peel and spoon the mixture into the prepared tin.

4. Bake for 30–40 minutes. The cake should be a deep golden colour and springy to the touch.

5. Cool in the tin for 15 minutes, then transfer to a cooling tray. Remove the paper after 5 minutes.

6. Make the icing by sifting the icing sugar into a small bowl and mixing in the lemon juice a tablespoon at a time until the icing is fairly runny.

7. Put the cake onto a serving plate and drizzle over the icing – it should fall down the sides of the cake and onto the plate. Sprinkle with some strips of lemon zest to serve.

FRUIT AND NUT CAKES
My Notes

4
Chocolate Cakes

Most people love chocolate cake of some kind – which is why in this chapter
I have included some of our family favourites that always get a cheer
whenever I make one. You will find all kinds of recipes here, everything from
straightforward cakes to cheesecakes and easy gateaux, so something
is sure to take the fancy of even the pickiest chocoholic.

All-in-one Chocolate Sandwich Cake

Use an electric mixer when making this recipe in order to make the best-quality cake. You can also use easy-spread butter here: it is softer and easier to mix into the other ingredients.

Makes about 8 portions

100g self-raising flour
50g cocoa powder
130g butter
130g golden caster sugar
2 eggs
4 tablespoons milk

For the filling
120g dark chocolate,
    broken into
    small pieces
2 tablespoons
    double cream
30g butter, very soft
30g icing sugar

For dusting
1 level tablespoon
    icing sugar
1 level tablespoon
    cocoa powder

1. Preheat the oven to 180°C/gas mark 4. Grease and line the bases of 2 x 18cm sandwich tins.

2. Put all the cake ingredients into a bowl and mix together with a mixer on its lowest setting.

3. When all the ingredients are combined, increase beating to the highest speed and continue to mix for 2–3 minutes. The mixture should look smooth and fluffy. Add a little more milk if the mixture doesn't fall readily from the spoon.

4. Divide the mixture between the prepared tins and bake for about 20 minutes, or until well risen and springy to the touch. Be careful not to overcook; it is difficult to tell just by looking at a chocolate cake whether it is baked or not, because the colour is misleading. Always test with your finger for springiness.

5. Leave to cool in the tins for 10 minutes, then transfer to a wire rack while you make the filling.

6. To make the filling, put the chocolate in a small heatproof bowl and add the cream. Place the bowl over a pan of very hot water and allow to melt. Stir very gently to combine.

7. Put the butter and icing sugar into a bowl and beat together until smooth and creamy.

9. When the chocolate has melted into the cream, cool and beat into the butter and sugar. Sandwich the cakes together, and finally, sieve the icing sugar and cocoa together over the top of the cake to finish.

White Chocolate Buns

A great addition to children's parties – or simply as an afternoon treat.

Make 12 large buns

100g butter
100g golden caster sugar
1 egg
100g self-raising flour
50g white
    chocolate chips
3 tablespoons milk

For the filling
170g white chocolate,
    chopped into
    small pieces
80ml double cream
90g butter
120g icing sugar

1–2 tablespoons icing
    sugar, for dusting

1. Preheat the oven to 170°C/gas mark 3. Put 12 muffin-sized paper cases in a 12-hole muffin tin.

2. Cream the butter and sugar together until fluffy and light. Beat in the egg.

3. Fold in the flour and chocolate chips, then stir in the milk.

4. Put a dessertspoonful of the mixture into each paper case and bake for 15 minutes, or until well risen and springy to the touch.

5. While the buns are cooling, make the filling: put the chocolate in a bowl with the cream and place over a bowl of hot water until the chocolate melts.

6. Beat the butter until light and soft, then beat in the icing sugar. Make sure the chocolate mixture isn't too hot and beat into the creamed mixture.

7. Cut a round out of the top of the cooled buns and put a generous teaspoon of the filling in each hole. Put the top back on and press down lightly.

8. Dust the tops with icing sugar.

Luxury Chocolate Cupcakes

I made these when my children were young. They all had (and still do have) their own ways of eating them: one ate the icing first while the others lift the icing off to eat the cake first. I am sure you will find your own way. They are worth the effort and go down well at children's parties, You can top the icing with their favourite sweets for an extra treat.

Makes 15 muffin-sized cupcakes

40g cocoa powder
140g self-raising flour
150g butter
150g golden caster sugar
3 eggs, beaten

For the icing
150g dark chocolate
2 tablespoons cream
50g butter
100g icing sugar

1. Preheat the oven to 180°C/gas mark 4. Put 15 muffin cases in two 12-hole muffin trays (put 8 in one and 7 in the other so they cook evenly).

2. Sieve the cocoa and flour together into a small bowl.

3. In a separate large mixing bowl, cream the butter and sugar until fluffy and light. Add 1 tablespoon of the flour and cocoa mixture and beat in the eggs gradually.

4. Sift in the rest of the flour and cocoa mixture and fold in with a large metal spoon.

5. Put a dessertspoonful of the cake mixture into each muffin case.

6. Bake for 15–20 minutes until well risen and springy to the touch. Allow to cool while you make the icing.

7. To make the icing, break the chocolate into small pieces into a heatproof bowl and add the cream. Place the bowl over a pan of hot water and allow to melt. Stir gently to mix the cream into the chocolate.

8. While the chocolate melts, whisk the butter and icing sugar together until light and soft. Allow the chocolate to cool for a few minutes, then whisk it into the icing mixture.

9. Put half a dessertspoonful of the chocolate icing on top of each cake and spread it out evenly.

10. Allow the icing to firm up before serving. Refrigerate the cupcakes for a quicker result.

Chocolate Fudge Cake

Choose this recipe any time you want a large, delicious cake on hand to impress your friends and family.

Serves 8

250g softened butter
200g golden caster sugar
50g ground almonds
230g self-raising flour
4 eggs
40g cocoa powder
60g dark chocolate, grated

For the fudge filling
160ml evaporated milk
120g soft brown sugar
120g dark chocolate
50g butter

1. Preheat the oven to 170°C/gas mark 3. Grease 2 x 22cm sandwich tins.

2. Cream the butter and sugar in a large mixing bowl until light and fluffy.

3. Add the ground almonds and a tablespoon of the flour and beat in the eggs gradually.

4. Sift the rest of the flour and cocoa together, then sift them again into the creamed mixture. Fold in with a metal spoon.

5. Divide the mixture between the sandwich tins and bake for 15–20 minutes, or until well risen and springy to the touch.

6. Leave to cool for 10 minutes in the tins, then transfer to a wire rack. The cakes must be completely cold before filling, so make the filling while they cool.

7. To make the filling, put the evaporated milk and sugar in a heavy-based pan over a low heat. Stir until all the sugar dissolves.

8. Bring the mixture to the boil, then immediately lower the heat and simmer for 3–4 minutes without stirring.

9. Remove from the heat and allow to cool for a couple of minutes, then stir in the chocolate and whisk it together.

10. Add the butter and whisk it into the mixture for 1 minute. Cool, cover and put the filling in the fridge to thicken. Once it has reached the desired consistency, beat with a wooden spoon and spread over the top of one layer.

11. Sandwich the layers together, then dust the top with a heaped teaspoon each of cocoa powder and icing sugar.

Chocolate Orange Cake

With its combination of chocolate and orange flavours, this cake doesn't disappoint.

Makes 10–12 portions

Zest and juice of 2
  medium oranges
40g demerara sugar
180g butter
130g soft brown sugar
50g cocoa
180g self-raising flour
3 eggs

For the orange topping
250g light soft
  cream cheese
80g icing sugar
Grated zest and juice
  of 1 orange

For decoration
Half a chocolate
  flake, crumbled
Crystallized or candied
  orange segments
  or peel: as many as
  you wish

1. Preheat the oven to 180°C/gas mark 4. Grease and line a 20cm square cake tin.

2. Put the orange zest and juice in a pan along with the demerara sugar. Stir over a low heat until all the sugar dissolves into the juice. Allow to go cold.

3. Cream the butter and brown sugar until light and fluffy. Sieve the cocoa and flour together and add a tablespoon to the creamed mixture, then gradually beat in the eggs.

4. Sift the rest of the flour into the creamed mixture in 3 lots. Using a metal spoon, fold in the flour and then a third of the cooled juice. Continue like this until all the flour and juice are incorporated.

5. Pour the mixture into the prepared tin and bake for 40–45 minutes until risen and springy to the touch.

6. Cool in the tin for 10 minutes, then transfer to a wire rack to cool completely before making the topping.

7. To make the topping, beat the cream cheese in a mixing bowl until soft and loose.

8. Beat in half of the icing sugar and the zest and juice.

9. Beat in the other half of the sugar for 2–3 minutes until smooth and spreadable. If the mixture is too stiff, add a little more orange juice.

10. Cut the cake in half horizontally and spread half of the cheese mixture over the surface of one half.

11. Sandwich the halves together, then spread the other half of the mixture over the top of the cake.

12. Decorate with the crumbled chocolate flake (or chocolate shavings) and candied orange segments.

Chocolate Marble Cake

Give this cake an extra-lovely shape by baking it in a brioche tin.

Make 8–10 portions

170g butter
170g golden caster sugar
3 eggs, beaten
170g self-raising flour
2 tablespoons
  cocoa mixed with
  2 tablespoons
  warm milk
100g icing sugar
50g dark chocolate,
  melted gently in
  a heatproof bowl
  over warm water

1. Preheat the oven to 180°C/gas mark 4. Grease a brioche tin.

2. Cream the butter and sugar in a mixing bowl until light and fluffy. Add 1 tablespoon of the flour and gradually beat in the eggs.

3. Sift the flour into the creamed mixture and fold in with a metal spoon.

4. Divide the mixture between 2 bowls. Add the cocoa mixture to 1 bowl and stir in carefully.

5. Alternately spoon each of the mixtures into the prepared tin, but don't mix them.

6. Bake for 20–25 minutes, or until well risen and springy to the touch.

7. Allow to cool for 10 minutes in the tin, then transfer to a wire rack.

8. Sift the icing sugar into a bowl and mix with a little water to make a thick, pourable icing.

9. Alternately drizzle the melted chocolate and icing over the top of the cake to give it a streaky, 'marbled' effect.

Variation
You can flavour this with coffee instead of chocolate: Mix 1½ rounded teaspoon of coffee granules with 2 tablespoons of hot water. Allow to cool and, at step 4, stir into the cake mixture instead of the cocoa powder. The colours are not as strikingly different as the chocolate but it is very tasty. Make 2 quantities of icing using 50g of icing sugar for each, and flavour one with coffee (made up as before) instead of water.

Chocolate-lover's Cheesecake

This is just what it says and can be eaten as a cake or a dessert. The chocolate chip cookies make a wonderful base for this luxurious-tasting cheesecake.

Serves 8

200g double chocolate
  chip cookies, crushed
100g unsalted
  butter, melted
1 egg
150g golden caster sugar
800g full-fat soft
  cream cheese
150g white chocolate,
  melted in a heatproof
  bowl over a pan
  of hot water
50g milk chocolate,
  melted as above

1. Mix the biscuit crumbs with the butter and press into the base of a buttered 22cm loose-bottomed tin. Place in the fridge for 30–40 minutes.

2. Preheat the oven to 150°C/gas mark 2.

3. Beat the egg and sugar into the cream cheese and stir in the melted white chocolate.

4. Pour the filling over the base.

5. Drizzle the melted milk chocolate into the filling and streak it with a skewer if you wish.

6. Bake for 1 hour and 20 minutes. When done, allow to cool in the tin completely before serving.

Chocolate Shortcake

This is in between a shortbread and a cake and can be cut into fingers if desired.

Makes 10–12 portions

130g butter
100g soft brown sugar
2 tablespoons chocolate
  drink granules
150g self-raising flour
50g plain flour

For the topping
100g dark chocolate
20g butter

1. Preheat the oven to 170°C/gas mark 3. Grease a shallow rectangular (tray-type) tin.

2. Cream the butter and sugar in a mixing bowl and fold in the chocolate granules. Sieve the flour into the creamed mixture and fold in.

3. Press into the prepared tin and bake for 20–25 minutes until risen and golden around the edges. Cool in the tin while you make the topping.

4. Melt the chocolate and butter in a bowl over hot water and stir gently. While still warm and fluid, spread the chocolate over the top of the shortcake.

5. Cut into the desired number of pieces when cool.

Chocolate Rum and Raisin Cake

This is a great cake to make around Christmas time for those who aren't fans of very rich fruit cake.

Makes 10 portions

100g raisins,
  roughly chopped
2–3 tablespoons rum
180g butter
150g soft brown sugar
200g self-raising flour
40g cocoa powder
2 eggs, beaten
150ml milk

For the icing
80g butter
120g icing sugar
1 tablespoon rum

50g dark
  chocolate, grated

1. Soak the raisins in the rum: use enough to coat the raisins without drenching them. Leave overnight.

2. Preheat the oven to 180°C/gas mark 4. Grease a 20cm round cake tin and line the base and sides with baking parchment.

3. Cream the butter and sugar in a bowl until the mixture is light and fluffy.

4. Sift the flour and cocoa powder together into a separate dish.

5. Sift a tablespoon of the flour and cocoa into the creamed mixture and beat in the eggs gradually. Fold in the rum-and-raisin mixture.

6. Sift in the flour and fold it in until it is just combined – don't worry if it's a bit streaky; this will sort itself out during baking. It is more important at this stage not to overmix; otherwise the air will escape and you will have a flatter cake.

7. Spoon the mixture into the prepared tin and smooth out the top, leaving a little well in the centre to allow for rising.

8. Bake for 40–45 minutes, or until the cake is well risen and springy to the touch. Allow to cool in the tin for 15 minutes, then transfer to a wire rack while you make the icing.

9. To make the icing, beat the butter to soften, then beat in the icing sugar until it becomes light and creamy.

10. Beat in the rum and spread on top of the cake smoothly. Top with the grated chocolate. To give it an extra-special finish, spread the top with two-thirds of the icing, then use a piping bag to pipe an edging around the cake with the rest.

Monster Jaffa Cake

For jaffa cake-lovers who dream of a huge version of their favourite snack. Some recipes call for a ready-made jelly, but this one tastes much better with its more authentic, orangey flavour.

Makes 8 portions

90g butter
90g caster sugar
90g self-raising flour
1 egg, beaten

For the orange jelly
1 large orange
15g powdered gelatine
400ml fresh orange juice

For the topping
200g dark chocolate

1. Preheat the oven to 170°C/gas mark 3. Grease and line a 22cm round, loose-bottomed shallow or sandwich tin.

2. Cream the butter and sugar in a large mixing bowl until pale and fluffy. Add a tablespoon of flour and beat in the egg.

3. Sift in the flour and fold into the mixture. Spoon into the prepared tin and bake for 15–20 minutes.

4. Allow to cool in the tin for 20 minutes then transfer to a wire rack.

To make the jelly
1. Grate the zest from the orange and put into a jug. Squeeze the juice into the jug; don't worry about the fleshy bits getting in – this adds to the flavour.

2. Add the gelatine, stir it into the zest and juice in the jug and leave to soften for 5–10 minutes.

3. Heat the 400ml of orange juice in a small pan until just hot. Remove from the heat. Pour the warmed juice into the juice-and-gelatine mixture and continue to stir for a few seconds to distribute the gelatine.

4. Pour the jelly into a 20cm greased sandwich tin. Leave to set firmly in the fridge. This will take an hour or 2.

To assemble the cake
1. Melt the chocolate topping in a bowl over very hot water. Put the sponge on a serving plate.

2. Loosen the jelly from the tin by dipping it in hot water to melt around the edges slightly, then tip it carefully on top of the sponge. The sponge should be slightly larger than the jelly.

3. Make a cardboard collar to go around the cake and secure it in place with a paper clip. Pour the melted chocolate over the top and allow to set for 1 hour in the fridge before removing the collar. This gives the cake a neat edge.

Sachertorte

This cake was first made in 1832 by Franz Sacher at the Hotel Sacher in Vienna. The original (and very secret) recipe is still made today, and the cakes are sent out all over the world. This version will keep in an airtight container for 2–3 days.

Makes 10–12 portions

200g dark chocolate, broken into small pieces
120g butter, softened
120g golden caster sugar
½ teaspoon vanilla extract
4 eggs, separated
120g plain flour
½ teaspoon baking powder
2 tablespoons apricot jam; this is easier to spread if you warm your spoon before spreading on to the cake

For the topping
200g dark chocolate
100ml double cream
1 dessertspoon golden syrup

1. Preheat the oven to 150°C/gas mark 2. Grease and line the base of a circular 20cm springform tin.

2. Melt the chocolate in a heatproof bowl over a pan of simmering water. While this melts, cream the butter, sugar and vanilla in a large mixing bowl.

3. Beat in the egg yolks, and when the chocolate has cooled, fold it into the creamed mixture.

4. Sift the flour and baking powder together onto a separate dish, then sift it again into the cake mixture. Fold in carefully.

5. In a clean bowl and using clean beaters, whisk the egg whites until they are stiff. Fold these into the cake mixture, adding a couple of tablespoons at a time.

6. Pour the mixture into the prepared tin and bake for 50–60 minutes. Don't overcook the cake or it will be dry. It is ready when it is firm to the touch yet well risen.

7. Allow to cool in the tin for 20 minutes, then transfer to a wire rack.

8. When completely cool, cut in half and spread the apricot jam over the centre, then sandwich the halves together.

9. Break the topping chocolate into small pieces and place in a bowl over hot water with the cream and syrup. Stir until the chocolate melts and the ingredients combine, then pour over the top of the cake.

10. Allow the topping to set before serving.

Variation
If you prefer, omit the syrup from the topping; this will make a firmer and less sweet icing.

Cherry and White Chocolate Gateau

A wonderful dinner party dessert or a cake for a special celebration.

Serves 6–8

150g butter
150g golden caster sugar
150g self-raising flour
3 eggs, beaten
50g white chocolate
  pieces or chips

For the filling
100ml whipping cream
20g white chocolate,
  broken into
  small pieces
20–25 cherries, pitted
  and soaked overnight
  in 4 tablespoons
  brandy or kirsch

For the topping
100g white chocolate
15g butter

For decoration
30g flaked almonds or
  grated chocolate
Fresh cherries for
  decoration (don't
  use soaked ones)

1. Preheat the oven to 180°C/gas mark 4. Grease and line 2 x 20cm cake tins. Tip: if you use the new silicone cake 'tins', you don't need to use lining paper, but I still grease them with a little butter.

2. Cream the butter and sugar until light and fluffy. Add 1 tablespoon of the flour and beat in the eggs.

3. Sieve in the rest of the flour, then fold it in with the chocolate pieces. Divide the mixture between the prepared tins.

4. Bake for 20 minutes, or until springy to the touch and golden in colour.

5. Leave to cool for 15 minutes in the tins, then transfer to a wire rack while you make the filling.

6. To make the filling, whip the cream until firm but not stiff, melt the chocolate in a heatproof bowl over a pan of very hot water, then fold it into the cream.

7. To make the topping, melt the chocolate and butter together in a bowl over a pan of very hot water or in a microwave.

To assemble the cake

1. Put one of the cake sections onto a serving plate and spread with the cream mixture. Squeeze the juice out of the cherries a little as you place them in the cream.

2. Put the second layer of cake carefully on the cherries and spread the top with the melted white chocolate.

3. Sprinkle the top with flaked almonds or grated chocolate and arrange the cherries in the centre, or wherever you think they look attractive.

4. Chill until ready to serve.

Variation
Turn this into a retro black forest gateau by using 2 tablespoons cocoa powder in the cake mixture, sieved in with the flour, and using dark chocolate whenever white is used.

CHOCOLATE CAKES
My Notes

5
Muffins

Muffins have become increasingly popular and my children love to eat and bake them themselves. They are very easy to make and can be flavoured with hundreds of different ingredients. We have just discovered savoury muffins from an American friend of ours, and they rival my favourite cheese scones.

The secret of making light and well risen muffins is not to overmix the flour and egg mixture. Simply mix everything together but don't worry about lumpy sections – the consistency will be fine once the muffins are baking because they almost mix themselves in the oven. Muffins bake at quite a high temperature, but again, this is necessary in order for them to rise well. If you've never made them before, however, check them after about 18 minutes so as not to burn them.

All the recipes in this chapter make about 12 large muffins, so put paper cases in a 12-hole muffin tray. Bake all muffins at 200°C/gas mark 6 unless otherwise stated.

The great thing about using fresh fruit in your muffins is that in most instances you don't need to cook it first (unless you wish to). In some cases you can even use use frozen and defrosted fruit, so these recipes can be made throughout the year – not just when the fruit is in season. Dried fruit and nuts are ideal for varying flavour; my particular favourite is the Orange, Sultana and Oat Muffin on page 77.

Muffins are best eaten soon after they are baked, but if you are keeping them for the next day, then heat them in the oven for five to six minutes at 200°C/gas mark 6, or for about 45 seconds in a microwave.

Classic Blueberry Muffins

I love the tangy berries in these muffins.

2 eggs
250ml milk
350g self-raising flour
Pinch of salt
80g golden caster sugar
100g soft brown sugar
120g butter, melted
180g blueberries, washed
 and dried

1. Preheat the oven to 200°C/gas mark 6.

2. Put the eggs in a mixing bowl. Add the milk and whisk together.

3. In a second mixing bowl, sift the flour and salt together and stir in the sugars.

4. Beat the melted butter into the egg mixture.

5. Pour the egg mixture into the flour and stir everything together fairly roughly. The flour may look a bit lumpy, but this is OK and won't make any difference to the finished muffins.

6. Stir in the blueberries.

7. Put a tablespoonful of the mixture into each case with about 1cm free at the top.

8. Bake for 20–25 minutes, or until well risen and springy to the touch.

Spicy Apple and Cinnamon Muffins

A wonderful autumn treat.

2 eggs
250ml milk
350g self-raising flour
1 teaspoon
  ground cinnamon
½ teaspoon
  ground ginger
¼ teaspoon
  grated nutmeg
2 tablespoons
  demerara sugar
120g butter, melted
180g dark brown sugar
2 Bramley apples, peeled,
  cored and diced
  (squeeze a little lemon
  juice over them to
  prevent browning)

1. Preheat the oven to 200°C/gas mark 6.

2. Beat the eggs and milk together in a jug.

3. Sift the flour and spices together into a large mixing bowl and stir in the sugar.

4. Stir the melted butter into the egg mixture and pour it into the flour. Mix together roughly.

5. Stir in the apples.

6. Put a tablespoon of the mixture into the muffin cases and top with a sprinkling of demerara sugar.

7. Bake for 20–25 minutes until springy to the touch.

Peach and Almond Muffins

If you wish to make these when peaches are out of season, use six canned halves in juice (not syrup) and drain well.

2 eggs
280ml milk
½ teaspoon
  almond extract
350g self-raising flour
180g soft brown sugar
50g ground almonds
20g chopped almonds
3 ripe medium peaches,
  peeled and diced
50g flaked almonds

1. Preheat the oven to 200°C/gas mark 6.

2. Beat the eggs, milk and almond extract together in a jug.

3. Sift the flour into a mixing bowl and stir in the sugar and ground and chopped almonds.

4. Pour in the egg mixture and stir to combine.

5. Stir in the peaches.

6. Put a tablespoon of the mixture into each muffin case and sprinkle some flaked almonds over the top of each muffin.

7. Bake for 20–25 minutes, or until risen and springy to the touch.

White Chocolate and Raspberry Muffins

2 eggs
250ml milk
1 teaspoon
  vanilla extract
350g self-raising flour
180g golden caster sugar
100g white chocolate
  broken into
  small pieces
120g melted butter
100g fresh or frozen and
  defrosted raspberries

1. Preheat the oven to 200°C/gas mark 6.

2. Beat the eggs, milk and vanilla together in a jug.

3. Sift the flour into a mixing bowl and stir in the sugar and chocolate pieces.

4. Stir the melted butter into the eggs.

5. Pour the egg mixture into the flour and stir to combine.

6. Stir in the raspberries.

7. Put a tablespoon of the mixture into the muffin cases and bake for 20–25 minutes, or until well risen and springy.

Orange, Sultana and Oat Muffins

I use about 200g tinned drained mandarin oranges for this recipe.

2 eggs
250ml milk
120g melted butter
330g self-raising flour
1 teaspoon
  baking powder
½ teaspoon allspice
180g golden caster sugar
50g oatmeal
100g sultanas
200g drained canned
  mandarin oranges,
  chopped roughly;
  retain the juice

1. Preheat the oven to 200°C/gas mark 6.

2. Beat the eggs and milk together and stir in the melted butter.

3. Sift the flour, baking powder and allspice into a mixing bowl.

4. Stir in the sugar and oatmeal.

5. Stir in the sultanas and orange pieces.

6. Pour the egg mixture amd 30ml of the retained orange juice into the flour and stir well to combine.

7. Put a tablespoon of the mixture into each muffin case and bake for 25-30 minutes.

Cherry and Almond Muffins

Try this recipe for a real taste of spring.

2 eggs
250ml milk
120g butter, melted
½ teaspoon
  almond extract
350g self-raising flour
50g chopped almonds
180g golden caster sugar
100g glacé cherries,
  halved or quartered
  if you prefer
50g flaked almonds,
  for the top

1. Preheat the oven to 200°C/gas mark 6.

2. Beat the eggs and milk in a jug and stir in the melted butter.

3. Stir in the almond extract.

4. Sieve the flour into a bowl and stir in the almonds and sugar.

5. Stir in the cherries.

6. Pour in the egg mixture and stir well to combine.

7. Put a tablespoon of the mixture into each muffin case and sprinkle the top with a few flaked almonds.

8. Bake for 25–30 minutes.

Banana Muffins

These are almost fat-free but are still very tasty. They don't keep fresh for as long as the ones that contain fats, but they can be warmed in the oven to freshen them up if necessary.

250g self-raising flour
½ teaspoon
   ground cinnamon
150g soft brown sugar
Approximately 220g
   bananas, mashed
60ml apple juice
2 eggs, beaten
100ml milk

1. Preheat the oven to 200°C/gas mark 6.

2. Sift the flour and cinnamon together into a bowl and stir in the sugar and bananas.

3. Beat the apple juice into the eggs. Stir in the milk and pour into the flour mixture. Stir everything together until just mixed.

4. Put a tablespoon of the mixture into each muffin case and bake for 20 minutes, or until well risen.

Variation
Stir 80g of chocolate chips into the flour after the sugar, before you add the bananas.

Carrot and Pecan Muffins

300g self-raising flour
½ teaspoon mixed spice
180g golden caster sugar
100g pecans,
    roughly chopped
1 Bramley apple, peeled,
    cored and diced
150ml sunflower oil
2 eggs
½ teaspoon vanilla extract
80ml milk
280g grated carrot

1. Preheat the oven to 200°C/gas mark 6.

2. Sift the flour and spice together into a large mixing bowl.

3. Stir in the sugar, then the nuts and apple.

4. Beat the oil into the eggs. Add the vanilla and stir in the milk. Add this to the flour mixture and stir to combine.

5. Stir in the carrots.

6. Spoon the mixture into the muffin cases and bake for 20–25 minutes.

Chocolate and Courgette Muffins

These go well with the cream cheese frosting, and they will keep for two to three days in a container in the fridge.

280g self-raising flour
3 tablespoons
    cocoa powder
150g soft brown sugar
50g raisins
1 beaten egg
90ml sunflower oil
90ml milk
½ teaspoon
    vanilla extract
300g courgettes, grated

For the frosting
120g cream cheese
30g crème fraîche
200g icing sugar

1. Preheat the oven to 200°C/gas mark 6.

2. Sift the flour and cocoa powder together in a mixing bowl.

3. Stir in the sugar and raisins.

4. In a separate bowl, whisk the egg, oil, milk and vanilla together.

5. Fold the egg mixture into the flour and stir in the courgettes.

6. Spoon the mixture into the muffin cases and bake for 20–25 minutes, or until springy to the touch.

7. To make the cream cheese frosting, whisk all the frosting ingredients together in a bowl; if it is too stiff, add a teaspoon of hot water. Spread over the top of the muffins to serve.

Peanut Butter Muffins

Using crunchy peanut butter works best in these muffins.

2 eggs
250ml milk
100g melted butter
350g self-raising flour
100g golden caster sugar
50g soft brown sugar
150g crunchy
   peanut butter

1. Preheat the oven to 200°C/gas mark 6.

2. Beat the eggs and milk together in a jug. Stir in the melted butter.

3. Sift the flour into a mixing bowl and stir in the sugars.

4. Use a knife to chop the peanut butter into the flour.

5. Pour the egg mixture into the flour and stir to combine.

6. Put a tablespoon of the mixture into each muffin case and bake for 25–30 minutes.

Variation
For a real American finish: heat 2–3 tablespoons of redcurrant jelly gently in a pan, brush the tops of the muffins with the warm jelly, then dip them into 50g chopped unsalted peanuts.

Savoury Muffins

These are great for breakfast or as an accompaniment to soup.

Cheddar Muffins

The chives add that special savoury taste to these delicious cheesy muffins.

2 eggs
250ml milk
120g butter, melted
320g self-raising flour
½ teaspoon salt
Pinch ground black
    pepper, or to taste
1 teaspoon dry
    mustard powder
200g mature
    Cheddar, grated
1 level tablespoon
    chopped fresh chives

1. Preheat the oven to 200°C/gas mark 6.

2. Beat the eggs and milk in a jug and stir in the melted butter.

3. Sieve the flour, salt, pepper and mustard together into a bowl.

4. Stir in the cheese (leaving a couple of tablespoons for the top) and the chives.

5. Pour in the egg mixture and stir to combine.

6. Put a dessertspoon of the mixture into the cases and sprinkle a little extra cheese on top of each.

7. Bake for 20–25 minutes, or until well risen and golden on top.

Variation
Fry 3 rashers of chopped bacon and stir into the dry ingredients along with the cheese.

Sun-dried Tomato and Black Olive Muffins

Full of sunny Mediterranean flavours.

2 eggs
250ml milk
120g butter, melted
320g self-raising flour
1 level teaspoon salt
¼ teaspoon black pepper
1 level teaspoon
  dried oregano
15–20 pitted black
  olives, chopped
100g sun-dried tomatoes
  in olive oil, drained
  of most of the oil
  and chopped
3 tablespoons
  grated Parmesan

1. Preheat the oven to 200°C/gas mark 6.

2. Beat the eggs and milk in a jug and stir in the melted butter.

3. Sieve the flour, salt and pepper into a mixing bowl and stir in the oregano.

4. Mix the olives and sun-dried tomatoes together and stir into the dry ingredients.

5. Pour in the egg mixture and stir to combine.

6. Put a dessertspoon of the mixture into each muffin case and sprinkle the Parmesan on top.

7. Bake for 20–25 minutes, or until well risen and golden brown.

Ham and Pineapple Muffins

A great muffin for a late breakfast or brunch.

2 eggs
250ml milk
120g butter, melted
320g self-raising flour
½ teaspoon salt
150g chopped
  cooked ham
100g canned crushed
  pineapple, drained

1. Preheat the oven to 200°C/gas mark 6.

2. Beat the eggs and milk in a jug and stir in the melted butter.

3. Sieve the flour and salt together into a large mixing bowl.

4. Stir in the ham and pineapple.

5. Pour the egg mixture into the flour and stir to combine.

6. Put a dessertspoon of the mixture into each muffin case.

7. Bake for 20–25 minutes until golden brown.

MUFFINS

My Notes.

6
Tray Bakes

Somehow, tray bakes seem less daunting to make than other baked goods, especially if you are just starting out on the baking journey. Many of these recipes are very easy to prepare and are much quicker than a cake.

Unless otherwise stated, most of the recipes in this chapter use an 18cm x 28cm rectangular tin that is about 3cm deep. For successful tray bakes, always butter or grease the tray well before baking, and if you prefer, line the base after greasing with baking parchment; this will make it easier to remove the bakes from the tray without breaking them.

Sticky Gingerbread

Perfect for ginger-lovers. Keep it in an airtight tin for 24 hours before eating.

Makes 16 squares

225g self-raising flour
1 teaspoon
    ground ginger
110g soft brown sugar
120g butter
1 tablespoon
    golden syrup
2 egg yolks (reserve
    the whites for the
    topping below)

For the topping
2 egg whites
2 tablespoons
    demerara sugar

1. Preheat the oven to 170°C/gas mark 3. Butter a rectangular tin.

2. Sieve the flour and ginger together into a large mixing bowl. Stir in the sugar.

3. Melt the butter and syrup together in a pan over a low heat. As soon as the butter has melted, remove from the heat and stir in the egg yolks.

4. Pour the butter mixture into the flour and stir well to combine all the ingredients.

5. Put the sticky dough into the prepared tin and press down well.

6. Brush the top of the dough with the egg white and sprinkle with the demerara sugar.

7. Bake for 30–35 minutes. Allow to cool for 15 minutes, then cut into squares.

Variations
• Add 50g of raisins or sultanas to the dry ingredients before adding the melted butter.

• If you really like ginger, use 25g chopped ginger in syrup as well as the ground ginger. Drain away any syrup before stirring into the melted butter.

Fruity Flapjacks

Flapjacks are a family favourite and these fruited ones are really delicious. This recipe keeps for five to six days in an airtight tin.

Makes 16–18 slices

150g butter
150g golden
   caster sugar
2 tablespoons
   golden syrup
330g porridge oats
100g raisins
50g sultanas
50g glacé cherries

1. Preheat the oven to 180°C/gas mark 4. Butter a rectangular tin.

2. Melt the butter, sugar and syrup in a large pan over a low heat.

3. Stir in the oats and dried fruit with a wooden spoon until fully combined, then press the mixture evenly into the prepared tin. Bake for 20–25 minutes.

4. Cut into the slices while they are still warm, but allow them to cool completely in the tin before removing them.

Variation
• For a real autumnal flavour around Bonfire Night, replace 1 tablespoon of syrup with 1 tablespoon of treacle or dark treacle.

Strawberry Oat Slice

This tray bake uses fresh strawberries, so for an economical treat, make it when they are cheap in season. You could also make it with fresh raspberries. It will keep for three to four days in an airtight tin.

Makes about 16 squares

400g strawberries,
   hulled and halved
120g golden caster sugar
300g porridge oats
100g butter

1. Preheat the oven to 200°C/gas mark 6. Butter a rectangular tin.

2. Mash the strawberries with the sugar in a mixing bowl. Stir in the oats and mix well.

3. Melt the butter in a pan over a low heat. Pour it over the oats and strawberry mixture and stir well with a wooden spoon. Press into the prepared tin.

4. Bake for 25 minutes.

5. Cut into 16 squares and leave to cool in the tin. When cold, pop in the fridge for 30 minutes before removing from the tin.

Triple Chocolate Brownies

Seriously chocolatey but very delicious, these will keep for four to five days in an airtight tin – if they last that long!

Makes 12

180g self-raising flour
20g cocoa powder
100g butter
200g soft brown sugar
2 tablespoons milk
1 large egg, beaten
50g white chocolate chips
100g dark chocolate,
   broken into
   small pieces

1. Preheat the oven to 180°C/gas mark 4. Butter a rectangular tin.

2. Sift the flour and cocoa powder into a mixing bowl.

3. Melt the butter and sugar together in a pan over a low heat, then pour into the flour mixture and beat well to combine.

4. Beat the milk into the egg, then add this to the dough mixture.

5. Stir in the chocolate chips and pieces. Mix everything thoroughly to form a soft, moist dough.

6. Press down into the tin and bake for 15–20 minutes. It is difficult to tell if brownies are baked just by looking, so press one with your finger; it should give but still remain flat if it is done.

7. Leave to cool in the tin for 20 minutes, then cut into 12 even pieces. Remove from the tin and transfer to a wire rack to cool completely.

Crunchy Slice

These are great fun for children to make. Add a little dried fruit or glacé cherries to the mixture for extra flavour. These will keep for three to four days in an airtight tin.

Makes 10–12

100g softened butter
150g soft brown sugar
1 beaten egg
150g self-raising flour
100g bar of dark
   chocolate, broken into
   small pieces (or dark
   chocolate chips)
50g crisped rice cereal

1. Preheat the oven to 180°C/ gas mark 4. Butter an 18cm square tin.

2. Cream the butter and sugar in a mixing bowl and beat in the egg. Fold in the flour, chocolate and cereal.

3. Press the mixture down lightly into the prepared tin and bake for 10–15 minutes.

4. Leave to cool for 15 minutes in the tin, then cut into slices or squares and transfer to a wire rack.

Luxury Muesli Slice

An extra-special muesli bar that is rich in fruit. They will keep for four to five days in an airtight container.

Makes 14–16 slices

200g butter
200g soft brown sugar
1 level teaspoon
   ground cinnamon
2 tablespoons honey
350g muesli
50g sultanas
50g raisins
50g glacé cherries,
   halved or quartered

1. Preheat the oven to 170°C/gas mark 3. Butter a rectangular tin.

2. Put the butter, sugar, cinnamon and honey together in a pan over a low heat. Stir to combine and dissolve the sugar.

3. Remove from the heat and stir in the muesli and dried fruit. Stir well so that all the muesli is coated in the butter mixture.

4. Spoon into the tin and press down evenly. Bake for 20–25 minutes.

5. Leave in the tin to cool completely, then use a sharp knife to cut into portions. Use a fish slice to lift out of the tin.

Variation
Pour 120g melted dark chocolate over the top and allow the chocolate to set before removing from the tin.

Golden Tray Bake

This is an easy and quick cake to make when your treat tins are empty.

Makes 8–10 portions

220g self-raising flour
180g butter, softened to
    room temperature
2 tablespoons
    golden syrup
80g soft brown sugar
2 eggs beaten with
    4 tablespoons milk
½–1 teaspoon
    vanilla extract
100g golden sultanas

1. Preheat the oven to 180°C/gas mark 4.

2. Sift the flour into a large mixing bowl.

3. Add all the other ingredients except for the sultanas. Using an electric mixer, start to mix all the ingredients together on the lowest speed setting.

4. When everything is beginning to combine, turn up to the next speed setting and beat for 2 minutes.

5. Finally, turn up to the fastest speed and continue to beat for another full minute. The mixture should look light and creamy.

6. Fold in the sultanas.

7. Spoon into the prepared tin and bake for 25–30 minutes, or until springy to the touch.

8. Allow to cool in the tin for 10 minutes, then cut into portions. Cool for 10 more minutes before transferring to a wire rack.

Paris Sandwich

This may be served as a teatime treat or as a pudding with custard or cream. Its shortbread-style layers are sandwiched together with jam.

Makes 10–12 portions

230g butter
350g plain flour
130g golden caster sugar
3–4 tablespoons jam
    of your choice

1. Preheat the oven to 180°C/gas mark 4. Butter a rectangular tin.

2. Rub the butter into the flour until the mixture resembles breadcrumbs. Stir in the sugar.

3. Bring the mixture together and knead lightly to make a smooth, pliable dough.

4. Divide the mixture into 2 equal parts and press 1 part into the prepared tin. Make sure it is thinly and evenly spread over the base of the tin. Don't take the dough up the sides, though.

5. Spread the jam over the base, leaving approximately 1.5cm edge all the way round. It will still seep out slightly, but don't worry.

6. Lightly flour a work surface and roll the other section of dough out to fit the top of the tin. Lay it carefully on top of the jam. Prick the top with a fork as you would a shortbread.

7. Bake for about 40 minutes, or until golden brown on top.

8. Allow to cool for 5 minutes, then cut into portions but leave in the tin. When cold, transfer to an airtight tin, where it will keep for 4–5 days.

Lemon Streusel Tray Bake

This is a recipe my mum made regularly because we all loved it. Sometimes she used jam or even marmalade, but mostly it was prepared using homemade lemon curd. This should keep fresh for up to four days if stored in an airtight tin.

Makes 8–10 portions

120g butter
80g golden caster sugar
150g plain flour
4–5 tablespoons
   lemon curd
   (or preserve of
   your choice)

For the topping
150g plain flour
½ teaspoon
   baking powder
120g butter
80g soft brown sugar
25g flaked or
   chopped almonds
Grated zest of 1 lemon

1. Preheat the oven to 180°C/gas mark 4. Butter a 20-22cm square tin.

2. Cream the butter and sugar in a mixing bowl until pale and fluffy.

3. Sift the flour into the creamed mixture and fold in.

4. Bring the dough together with your hands, kneading lightly, then press it evenly into the base of the tin.

5. Bake for 15 minutes until lightly cooked. Allow to cool for 10 minutes while you make the topping.

6. Sieve the flour and baking powder together into a mixing bowl, then rub in the butter until the mixture looks like breadcrumbs.

7. Stir in the sugar, almonds and lemon zest.

8. Spread lemon curd evenly over the shortbread base, then sprinkle on the topping, but don't be tempted to press it down.

9. Bake for 25–30 minutes until the top is golden in colour.

10. Cool for 10 minutes in the tin, then cut into potions. Leave to cool completely before removing from the tin.

Apple and Date Slice

This is a tasty mixture of a crunchy base, stewed apple and a crumbly yet crispy top. It takes a little more preparation than many of the other recipes in this chapter, but it is still easy to make – and well worth the effort.

Makes 8–10 portions

For the filling
2 cooking apples, peeled, cored and diced
1 tablespoon lemon juice
3 tablespoons apple juice
4 tablespoons orange juice
2 tablespoons honey
200g chopped dates
Grated zest of 1 orange

For the base
110g self-raising flour
½ teaspoon ground cinnamon
A pinch of grated nutmeg
80g wholemeal flour
2 tablespoons soft brown sugar
150g butter
100g porridge oats
2 tablespoons honey
1 egg, beaten

1. Stew the apples, fruit juices and 1 tablespoon of the honey together in pan until the apples are smooth.

2. Add the dates, the rest of the honey and the orange zest. Cook gently for about 5 minutes, or until the dates soften. Leave to cool.

3. Butter a rectangular tin.

4. To make the base, sieve the self-raising flour and spices together in a mixing bowl. Stir in the wholemeal flour and the sugar.

5. Rub the butter into the flours and sugar mixture until it resembles breadcrumbs. Stir in the oats.

6. Drizzle in the honey and beaten egg and stir well with a wooden spoon until the mixture is well-combined. It should be soft and pliable.

7. Press two-thirds of the mixture into the base of the tin, making sure it is spread evenly. Roll the other piece of dough into a ball and wrap in cling film. Place in the freezer for 30 minutes.

8. Preheat the oven to 180°C/gas mark 4. Spread the cooled filling over the base.

9. Grate the dough from the freezer evenly over the top of the apple mixture. Press down lightly.

10. Bake for 25–30 minutes, or until golden brown.

11. Leave in the tin to cool for 10 minutes, then cut into slices. Once cold, remove from the tin and store in an airtight container, where it will keep for 3–4 days.

No-bake Chocolate Slice

This is a cheat, really, as it shouldn't be in a baking book: you don't bake it at all. But it is a real treat for chocolate-lovers. It is also useful if your bourbon biscuits have perhaps gone a little stale because you can use them up in this recipe. This should keep fresh for about seven days in an airtight container.

Makes 12–14 portions

250g bourbon biscuits, crushed finely
50g glacé cherries, halved
50g desiccated coconut
30g walnuts, roughly chopped
1 tablespoon cocoa powder
100g dark chocolate, broken into small pieces
80g butter
1 tablespoon golden syrup
1 egg, beaten
50g white chocolate, to decorate (optional)

1. Butter a 30cm x 20cm rectangular tin.

2. Put the biscuits, cherries, coconut and walnuts into a bowl and sift the cocoa over the top. Stir everything well together.

3. Put the chocolate, butter and syrup in a pan over a very low heat and allow everything to melt together, stirring occasionally. Remove from the heat as soon as the chocolate has melted.

4. Make a well in the centre of the dry ingredients and pour in the chocolate mixture. Before stirring, add the beaten egg and mix together with a wooden spoon.

5. Press the mixture down well into the prepared tin and refrigerate for about 45 minutes.

6. Cut into small pieces as it is very rich. Remove from the tin using a fish slice. Decorate with melted white chocolate drizzled over the top if you wish.

Caribbean Squares

An unusual slice that combines coconut, pineapple and a little Malibu. The latter is optional, however.

Makes 8–10

250g oatmeal-type
  biscuits, finely crushed
60g desiccated coconut
200g fresh (or well-
  drained canned)
  pineapple, cut into
  small pieces
100g ground almonds
180ml condensed milk
20ml Malibu
100g butter, melted

For the icing
50g butter
150g icing sugar
1 tablespoon
  coconut cream
1 tablespoon
  desiccated coconut
25g glacé pineapple,
  to decorate

1. Preheat the oven to 180°C/gas mark 4. Butter a rectangular tin.

2. Put the biscuits, coconut, pineapple and almonds into a large mixing bowl and stir well.

3. Make a well in the centre and add the condensed milk, Malibu and melted butter. Stir well until it all combined.

4. Press down in the prepared tin.

5. Bake for 20 minutes, or until the top is pale gold. Allow to cool while you make the icing.

6. Cream the butter in a mixing bowl until soft.

7. Sift in the icing sugar and beat well.

8. Beat in the creamed and desiccated coconut.

9. Smooth over the top of the slice and decorate with the glacé pineapple.

10. Cut into portions and store in an airtight tin. This should keep for 4 days.

Cherry and Coconut Slice

This is made in a shallow Swiss-roll-type tin. Butter it well.

Makes about 16 portions

150g self-raising flour
80g desiccated coconut
60g golden caster sugar
120g butter, melted
120g glacé
  cherries, chopped
30g soft brown sugar
80g desiccated coconut
2 eggs, beaten
50g dark chocolate

1. Preheat the oven to 180°C/gas mark 4. Butter a shallow 30cm x 20cm tin.

2. Sift the flour into a bowl and stir in the coconut and sugar.

3. Stir in the melted butter and mix to make a soft dough. Press the mixture into the prepared tin.

4. In a clean bowl combine the cherries, sugar and coconut. Add the beaten eggs and stir well. Spread this mixture over the base.

5. Bake for about 20 minutes, or until golden brown.

6. While the slice is cooling, melt the chocolate in a heatproof bowl over a pan of hot water and drizzle it over the top in a crisscross pattern. Allow the chocolate to set before cutting into portions.

Lemon Fingers

These treats have a buttery base and are topped with a refreshing lemon-custardy topping. Try making it with oranges instead of lemons for a change.

Makes 16–18 portions

100g plain flour
80g self-raising flour
180g icing sugar
180g butter; remove
    from the fridge just
    before use and cut
    into small pieces
Grated zest of 1 lemon

For the topping
4 eggs
350g caster sugar
100ml fresh lemon juice
Grated zest of 1 lemon
180ml double cream
1 tablespoon icing sugar,
    for dusting

1. Preheat the oven to 170°C/gas mark 3. Butter a rectangular tin.

2. Sift the 2 flours and icing sugar together into a large mixing bowl.

3. Add the butter and lemon zest and rub in with your fingertips until the mixture resembles breadcrumbs. Work the dough until it comes together in a ball.

4. Press this down evenly into the prepared tin.

5. Bake for about 15–20 minutes until it has turned a light golden colour.

6. Make the topping while the base cools: put the eggs and sugar into a mixing bowl and beat until light and fluffy. This will take about 4 minutes by hand or 2 minutes using an electric whisk.

7. Beat the lemon juice and zest into the egg mixture.

8. In a separate bowl, whip the cream until it forms soft peaks. Fold it into the egg mixture one-half at a time.

9. Pour the cream and egg mixture over the top of the base.

10. Bake for about 40 minutes, or until the topping is set and beginning to colour.

11. Allow to cool completely in the tin, then cut into fingers and dust the tops with icing sugar.

12. When storing this in an airtight tin, do so in single layers as it will stick together otherwise. It should keep for 3–4 days.

Coffee Fudge Bars

So easy and great for coffee addicts, these gooey, delicious bars will keep for four to five days.

Makes 12–14 bars

150g butter
100g dark brown sugar
180g self-raising flour
1 rounded teaspoon
   coffee granules mixed
   with 2 tablespoons
   of hot water

For the icing
120g icing sugar
1 level teaspoon coffee
   granules mixed with
   2 teaspoons of
   hot water
60g butter
2 teaspoons icing sugar,
   for dusting

1. Preheat the oven to 180°C/gas mark 4. Grease a 30cm x 20cm Swiss roll tin.

2. Cream the butter and sugar in a mixing bowl until light and fluffy.

3. Sift the flour into the creamed mixture and fold in. Add the coffee and stir in.

4. Spoon the mixture into the prepared tin and bake for 15–20 minutes, or until springy to the touch. Cool in the tin for 20 minutes.

5. Put all the icing ingredients into a pan over a low heat. Stir constantly until the butter has melted and the icing has become thick and smooth, then beat for 2 minutes away from the heat.

6. Spread the icing over the bars; use a metal palette knife to smooth it out. Dust with icing sugar, allow to set, then cut into bars. Store in an airtight container.

Mixed Nut and Maple Slice

This tray bake may also be made with mixed nuts or just peanuts if you prefer. Use real maple syrup as it gives a truer flavour in the cake; it is a bit more expensive but worth it.

Makes 12–14 portions

110g butter, at
   room temperature
110g soft light brown
   sugar
4 tablespoons
   peanut butter
4 tablespoons
   maple syrup
110g self-raising flour
2 eggs, beaten
120g mixed chopped
   nuts (or chopped
   peanuts)

1. Preheat the oven to 180°C/gas mark 4. Grease and line the base of a 23cm square cake tin.

2. Cream the butter and sugar in a mixing bowl until light and fluffy.

3. Add the peanut butter and maple syrup and beat into the butter mixture.

4. Sift a tablespoon of the flour over the mixture and beat in the eggs gradually.

5. Sift in the rest of the flour and fold in with a metal spoon, adding the nuts as you fold in the flour. Keep about 20g of the nuts to sprinkle on top.

6. Spoon the mixture into the prepared tin and sprinkle the top with the nuts.

7. Bake for 30–35 minutes until springy to the touch.

8. Cool in the tin for 10 minutes, then cut into portions before transferring to a wire rack. This will keep for about 4–5 days in an airtight container.

Iced Rich Fruit Slice

This shallow fruit cake is great for those who like small portions, and is ideal for Christmas with a festive glass of sherry or port. It requires just 24 hours to mature, and can be skewered and drizzled with two or three tablespoons of brandy or rum before icing, if desired.

Make about 12–14 portions

160g butter
160g soft brown sugar
220g plain flour
1 teaspoon
  baking powder
1 teaspoon mixed spice
½ teaspoon
  ground cinnamon
50g ground almonds
3 eggs, beaten
100g raisins
100g sultanas
100g currants
50g glacé cherries,
  quartered
30g mixed candied
  peel (or the
  equivalent measure
  of glacé cherries)
Grated zest of 1 lemon
2 tablespoons sieved
  apricot jam
450g marzipan
  (see page 11)

For the icing
500g icing sugar
3 egg whites
½ teaspoon lemon juice

1. Preheat the oven to 150°C/gas mark 2. Grease and line a 30cm x 20cm x 3cm baking tin. Leave a 'grabbing edge' so the cake will be easy to lift out.

2. Cream the butter and sugar in a large mixing bowl. Sift the flour, baking powder and spices into a second mixing bowl and stir in the almonds.

3. Add a tablespoon of the flour mixture to the creamed mixture and a third of the egg. Beat well. Repeat this with a tablespoon of flour then a second third of the egg and beat. Repeat a third time.

4. Combine all the fruit in a bowl with the lemon zest. Add half of the rest of the flour and fold into the creamed mixture. Fold in half of the fruit, then the rest of the flour. Finally, finish folding in the fruit mixture.

5. Spoon into the prepared tin; the mixture should come quite near the top.

6. Bake for 30 minutes, then turn the heat down to 140°C/gas mark 1 for another 30–40 minutes. If it is browning too quickly, cover with a sheet of foil. Test for doneness by pushing a skewer in the centre; it should come out clean.

7. Cool for 20 minutes in the tin, then carefully lift out onto a wire rack with the paper still attached. Remove the paper when completely cold. Wrap in greaseproof paper and leave in an airtight container for about 24 hours.

8. Brush the top of the cake with apricot jam. Dust a work surface with icing sugar and roll out the marzipan quite thinly. Fit it over the top and at least halfway down the sides of the cake. Leave to dry for 2 hours.

9. Make the icing by sifting the icing sugar into a bowl. Beat in the egg whites and lemon juice vigorously until the mixture forms stiff peaks. Spread evenly over the marzipan and smooth out with a palette knife; it doesn't have to look perfectly smooth. To peak the icing, let it set for about 20 minutes, then use the back of a spoon to pull the icing up gently into peaks. The icing will take about 12 hours to set completely.

10. Store in an airtight tin for 3–4 weeks.

TRAY BAKES
My Notes

Biscuits

The word *biscuit* comes from the French *bis cuit*, which means 'baked again', because some of the earliest biscuits were baked once to preserve them, then again just before eating. A true biscuit is one that makes a snapping sound when broken in half; if it doesn't do this, it should technically be called a cookie – in the sense that the word originally meant 'little cake'. But don't worry about this: some of my cookies snap and some of my biscuits don't! Shops sell really good biscuits these days, but they are very expensive. I have found that you can make your own basic, family and luxury biscuits for a fraction of the price – and also, they actually taste better. The best news is that they are generally not difficult to bake and can be made quickly and easily.

The secret of baking biscuits is not to overcook them and always to be aware of the length of time they are in the oven.

Shortbread

This is our family favourite. There are two methods of preparation; both are given here and produce an excellent result. Whichever you use, the shortbread will keep for six to seven days when stored in an airtight tin.

Makes 10–14 portions

100g self-raising flour
100g plain flour
130g softened butter
100g golden caster sugar

The Rubbed-in Method

This method is for those who like making pastry and using their fingers to incorporate the ingredients.

1. Preheat the oven to 180°C/gas mark 4. Grease a 20cm round sandwich tin or an 18cm x 28cm rectangular tin.

2. Sift the flours into a mixing bowl. Cut the butter into small pieces and add these to the flour. Rub the butter into the flour until the mixture is fine and looks like breadcrumbs.

3. Sprinkle in the sugar and stir well.

4. Bring the mixture together with your hands and knead lightly until a smooth dough is formed.

5. Press the dough down into the tin so that it is evenly distributed. Prick all over with a fork, leaving a 2cm edge.

6. Bake for 25–30 minutes until golden brown.

7. Leave in the tin to cool, but cut into 14 finger-sized pieces while the shortbread is warm. Lift out when completely cool and store in an airtight tin.

The Creaming Method

You can use an electric hand mixer to prepare this, so it is easier on the hands.

1. Preheat the oven to 180°C/gas mark 4. Grease a 20cm round sandwich tin or an 18cm x 28cm rectangular tin.

2. Cream the butter and sugar together in a mixing bowl until light and fluffy.

3. Sift the flours together into the creamed mixture and mix in with a wooden spoon.

4. Use your hands to bring the mixture to a ball and knead it lightly until it forms a smooth dough. Follow steps 5, 6 and 7 in the previous method.

Variations

• Stir in 80g halved glacé cherries with the sugar in the first method, or with the sieved flour in the second.

• To make chocolate shortbread, substitute 20g cocoa powder for 20g of plain flour in both methods.

• For iced shortbread, when cool, spread glacé icing over the top with a palette knife. Simply mix 100g sifted icing sugar with enough water to make a thick but spreadable icing.

Walnut Biscuits

These will keep for five to seven days in an airtight tin.

Makes about 25

125g butter
110g golden caster sugar
1 egg, beaten
10g plain flour
50g self-raising flour
2 level teaspoons
 cinnamon
1 tablespoon
 cocoa powder
50g chopped walnuts
Walnut halves,
 for decoration
Icing sugar,
 for dusting

1. Preheat the oven to 180°C/gas mark 4. Grease 2 baking sheets.

2. Cream the butter and sugar in a mixing bowl until light and soft. Add the egg and beat in well.

3. Sieve together the flours, cinnamon and cocoa powder.

4. Add the chopped walnuts, then a little of the flour mixture and fold in. Continue folding in the flour until it is all incorporated.

5. Bring the mixture together with your hands. Break off small pieces and roll them into balls, then lightly press them down onto the baking sheet. Place a whole or half of a walnut into the centre of each biscuit.

6. Bake for 10–12 minutes.

7. Cool for a few minutes on the baking sheet, then transfer to a wire rack. Dust with a little icing sugar before serving.

Wheaten Biscuits

These semi-sweet biscuits can be served with cheese. The thinner you roll out the dough, the crisper the biscuits.

Makes about 20

130g softened butter
80g golden caster sugar
1 whole egg and
    1 egg yolk
150g whole wheat flour
75g plain white flour
A pinch of salt

1. Preheat the oven to 180°C/gas mark 4. Grease 2 baking sheets.

2. Cream butter and sugar in a mixing bowl and beat in the eggs. The mixture should be light and soft.

3. Sieve the flours together along with the salt. Add to the creamed mixture, folding in gradually.

4. When all the flour is incorporated, bring the mixture together to form a dough.

5. Roll out the dough to about 1cm thick on a clean, lightly floured surface. Cut into rounds and place on the prepared baking sheets.

6. Bake for 10–15 minutes and allow to cool on the baking sheet for a few minutes before transferring to a wire rack.

Anzac Biscuits

These biscuits have long been associated with Australian and New Zealand soldiers from World War I, when they were sent to the troops as presents from loved ones. They kept well during the long transportation.

Makes about 24

150g plain flour
150g caster sugar
60g oats
60g desiccated coconut
130g butter
2 tablespoons
  golden syrup
1 tablespoon honey
1 tablespoon
  boiling water
½ teaspoon
  baking powder

1. Preheat the oven to 180°C/gas mark 4. Grease 2 baking sheets.

2. Sift the flour into a mixing bowl and stir in the sugar. Stir in the oats and coconut.

3. Put the butter in a pan over a low heat and add the syrup and honey. As the butter melts, stir well to combine.

4. Add the boiling water to the baking powder, then pour this into the butter and syrup mixture.

5. Make a well in the dry ingredients, then add the butter mixture. Stir well with a wooden spoon until everything is combined.

6. Put a dessertspoonful of the mixture onto the baking sheet and flatten with the back of the spoon. Do this with all the mixture, allowing about 2cm between each biscuit.

7. Bake for 15–20 minutes, or until golden brown.

8. Transfer the biscuits to a wire rack to cool completely, then store in an airtight container. They should keep for 6–7 days.

Melting Moments

These are exactly what they say: they really do melt in your mouth. They'll keep for four to five days in an airtight container – but they probably won't last that long!

Makes 15–20

100g softened butter
80g golden caster sugar
1 egg, beaten
4–5 drops vanilla extract
150g self-raising flour
75g rolled oats
glacé cherries, halved

1. Preheat the oven to 180°C/gas mark 4. Grease a baking sheet.

2. Cream the butter and sugar in a mixing bowl until light and fluffy. Beat in the egg and vanilla.

3. Fold in the flour and bring the dough together with your hands.

4. Roll small pieces of the dough into balls, then roll these in the oats.

5. Place onto the baking sheet and press down to form a round. Space the biscuits about 2cm apart to allow for spreading.

6. Put half a glacé cherry on top of each biscuit and bake for 10–15 minutes.

7. Leave on the baking sheet to cool for 15 minutes before transferring to a wire rack.

Chocolate and Peanut Butter Cookies

Even if you're not too keen on peanut butter, you will love these chocolatey cookies.

Makes 15–20

100g butter
120g soft brown sugar
120g plain flour
200g smooth
   peanut butter
1 egg, beaten
2 tablespoons
   cocoa powder
½ teaspoon
   baking powder

For the topping
50g dark chocolate
A small knob of butter

1. Cream the butter and the sugar in a mixing bowl until fluffy.

2. Add 1 tablespoon of the flour and the peanut butter and beat in well.

3. Beat in the egg.

4. Sieve the rest of the flour with the cocoa powder and baking powder and fold into the rest of the mixture.

5. Use your hands, as cold as possible, to combine the dough and knead for a few seconds. Roll it into a ball, wrap it in greaseproof paper and chill it in the fridge for 1 hour.

6. While the dough is chilling, preheat the oven to 190°C/gas mark 5 and place a piece of baking paper on 2 baking sheets.

7. Once it has chilled, cut off small amounts of the dough and roll these lightly in your hands to form balls. Put them on the baking sheet and press down to form a flat disc.

8. Bake for 12–15 minutes. Cool on the baking sheet for 10 minutes, then transfer to a wire rack.

9. Melt the chocolate and butter together in a heatproof bowl over a pan of hot water and drizzle over the biscuits to finish.

Coffee and Hazelnut Biscuits

Makes 20–22

100g butter
100g golden caster sugar
3 teaspoons coffee
  granules mixed with
  3 teaspoons
  boiling water
1 egg yolk
190g plain flour
50g ground hazelnuts
50g chopped hazelnuts

For the icing
80g icing sugar
½ teaspoon coffee
  granules mixed
  with 1 teaspoon
  boiling water
2–3 teaspoons milk
Extra chopped hazelnuts,
  for decoration

1. Cream the butter and sugar in a mixing bowl until fluffy.

2. Beat in the coffee and the egg yolk.

3. Sieve the flour into the creamed mixture and fold in.

4. Stir in both kinds of nuts and make sure they are well combined, without overbeating.

5. Knead with the hands lightly to form a smooth ball.

6. Put the dough onto a lightly floured surface and roll into a long sausage shape measuring about 28cm long and 4cm in diameter.

7. Wrap the dough in cling film and put it in the freezer for 30 minutes.

8. Preheat the oven to 180°C/gas mark 4 and line 2 baking sheets with baking paper.

9. Cut the cold dough into about 20–22 discs and place them on the baking sheets about 3cm apart.

10. Bake for 15–20 minutes, or until golden, and leave to cool for 15 minutes on the tray before transferring them to a wire rack.

11. Make the icing by sieving the icing sugar into a bowl and beating in the coffee and milk to make a spreadable icing.

12. Spread a thin layer over the biscuits and top with a sprinkling of the extra hazelnuts.

Almond Macaroons

These are very light and crisp. They make a good accompaniment to coffee after a meal, and should keep for two to three days in an airtight container.

Makes 18–20

100g ground almonds
180g golden caster sugar
1 rounded teaspoon
    plain flour
2 egg whites
½ teaspoon
    almond extract
20g chopped almonds

1. Preheat the oven to 180°C/gas mark 4. Line 2 baking sheets with baking paper.

2. Put the almonds and sugar into a bowl and stir together. Sift the flour into the bowl and stir well.

3. Add the egg whites and almond extract and beat or whisk until combined.

4. Drop teaspoons of the mixture onto the baking sheets, leaving about 3cm between each one.

5. Sprinkle a few chopped almonds onto the top of each biscuit.

6. Bake for 15–20 minutes. Cool on the tray for 5 minutes, then transfer to a wire rack.

Chocolate-dipped Coconut Macaroons

They're delicious with or without, but these macaroons become extra-special when dipped in dark chocolate.

Makes 8–10

250g desiccated coconut
50g ground almonds
150ml condensed milk
½ teaspoon
  vanilla extract
2 egg whites

For the chocolate coating
100g dark chocolate
A knob of butter

1. Preheat the oven to 180°C/gas mark 4. Line 2 large baking sheets with baking paper.

2. Put the coconut, almonds, condensed milk and vanilla extract in a bowl and stir well with a wooden spoon to combine. The mixture should be moist but not runny; add a little more coconut if it isn't holding together.

3. Put the egg whites in a bowl and whisk until stiff. Fold 1 tablespoon into the coconut mixture to loosen, then add the rest gradually, folding it in.

4. Drop the mixture a tablespoon at a time onto the baking sheet, spacing them about 3cm apart.

5. Bake for about 15 minutes until golden and firm on the outside. Leave to cool on the tray for 10 minutes, then transfer to a wire rack.

6. Melt the chocolate and butter in a heatproof bowl placed over a pan of hot water. When the macaroons are cool, dip half (or all) into the chocolate and place on a piece of greaseproof paper. Leave to set in a cool place.

Florentines

These very elegant biscuits are a real treat. They will keep for two to three days in an airtight tin but are best eaten as soon as possible.

Makes 12–14

50g plain flour
30g chopped walnuts
30g flaked almonds
30g chopped
  glacé cherries
30g raisins
80g butter
50g soft brown sugar
200g dark chocolate,
  broken into
  small pieces

1. Preheat the oven to 180°C/gas mark 4. Line 2 baking sheets with baking paper.

2. Sift the flour into a mixing bowl. Stir in the nuts and fruit.

3. Melt the butter and sugar in a small pan over a low heat and stir well until the sugar has dissolved.

4. Stir the butter mixture into the dry ingredients. Don't overstir or the nuts will lose their texture.

5. Drop the mixture a dessertspoonful at a time onto the baking sheets, leaving about 5cm between each one. Press each down gently with the back of a spoon to form a round.

6. Bake for about 8 minutes, then remove from the oven. Press down again if necessary to form a round with a palette knife. Leave to cool on the baking sheet for 5 minutes, then transfer to a wire rack.

7. Melt the chocolate in a heatproof bowl placed over a pan of simmering water.

8. As soon as the chocolate is fully melted, use the palette knife to coat one side of the Florentines thickly. Allow to set.

Viennese Biscuits

Viennese biscuits come in a variety of shapes, but here are two favourites; both should keep for three to four days in an airtight tin. You will need a piping bag fitted with a star-shaped nozzle to make these.

Makes 12–24, depending on shape

150g butter
50g icing sugar
½ teaspoon
   vanilla extract
150g plain flour
80g dark chocolate,
   for dipping

1. Preheat the oven to 180°C/gas mark 4. Grease a large baking sheet.

2. Put the butter into a mixing bowl and cream until soft.

3. Sift in the icing sugar and cream it with the butter.

4. Add the vanilla and beat into the mixture.

5. Sift in the flour and fold into the creamed mixture to make a soft dough.

To make Viennese Fingers
1. Put the dough into a piping bag and pipe fingers about 2cm apart onto the baking sheet.

2. Bake for 15–20 minutes. Remove and allow to cool for 5 minutes on the tray, then transfer to a wire rack.

3. Melt the dark chocolate in a heatproof bowl placed over a pan of simmering water.

4. Dip each biscuit into the chocolate so half is covered and allow to set.

To make Viennese Whirls
1. Put the dough in a piping bag and pipe circular whirls onto the baking sheet.

2. Bake for 15–20 minutes. Allow to cool for 5 minutes, then transfer to a cooling rack.

3. When cool, sandwich together with a blob of raspberry jam and a teaspoon of buttercream – see page 8.

Pinwheels

These look very difficult to make, but in fact are easy and fun. You will need to make two lots of dough: one vanilla-flavoured and one flavoured with cocoa. These should keep for about three to four days in an airtight tin.

Makes 18–20

For the vanilla dough
80g butter
150g golden
    caster sugar
1 egg
½ teaspoon
    vanilla extract
180g plain flour

For the chocolate dough
80g butter
150g golden caster sugar
1 egg
160g plain flour
20g cocoa powder

1. Make the vanilla dough by creaming the butter and sugar in a large mixing bowl.

2. Add the egg and vanilla, and beat into the creamed mixture.

3. Sift in the flour and stir, first with a wooden spoon, then knead lightly with your hands until well combined.

4. Make the chocolate dough in the same way, but sieve the flour and cocoa together first before sifting again into the creamed mixture.

5. Roll out the vanilla dough on a sheet of baking paper until it measures approximately 32cm x 24cm. If the dough is too soft to roll, sprinkle on a little flour as you roll out. Do the same with the chocolate dough until it measures the same as the vanilla dough.

6. Carefully place the chocolate dough on top of the vanilla.

7. Use the baking paper under them to help roll into a tight, long sausage shape the length of the longest side.

8. Roll the dough in the baking paper and chill for 1½–2 hours hours in the fridge.

9. Preheat the oven to 180°C/gas mark 4. Grease 2 baking sheets.

10. Remove the dough from the fridge and cut into slices to make round, flat shapes. They will look like pinwheels.

11. Lay them on the baking sheet positioned about 3cm apart and bake for 10–15 minutes.

12. Allow to cool for 5 minutes on the tray, then transfer to a wire rack to cool completely.

Parkin Biscuits

These rich ginger and oat biscuits taste like parkin (see page 31), but are crispy on the outside and chewy in the centre. They will taste even better if you store them for 24 hours in an airtight container before eating, and should keep for six to seven days.

Makes 14–18

120g butter
100g dark brown sugar
1 tablespoon
   dark treacle
1 tablespoon
   golden syrup
150g plain flour
½ teaspoon
   ground ginger
½ teaspoon
   ground cinnamon
20g ground almonds
150g oatmeal

1. Preheat the oven to 180°C/gas mark 4. Line 2 baking sheets with baking paper.

2. Put the butter, sugar, treacle and syrup into a pan over a low heat and allow everything to melt together, stirring gently while the sugar dissolves.

3. Sift the flour and spices together into a large bowl. Stir in the almonds and oatmeal.

4. Make a well in the centre of the dry ingredients and pour in the butter mixture. Mix thoroughly with a wooden spoon.

5. Put small spoonfuls of the mixture onto the baking sheets, leaving about 3cm gap between each.

6. Bake for 10–12 minutes. Leave to cool for 5 minutes on the sheets, then transfer to a wire rack.

Brandy Snaps

This recipe can be used to make the traditional brandy snap tubes or little baskets to hold fruit and cream or custard. They make ideal dessert bases.

Makes 8–10

60g butter
60g caster sugar
60g golden syrup
60g plain flour
½ teaspoon
   ground ginger
2 teaspoons lemon juice
1 teaspoon brandy,
   optional

1. Preheat the oven to 180°C/gas mark 4. Line 2 large baking sheets with baking paper.

2. Put the butter, sugar and syrup into a pan over a low heat and allow the butter to melt. Stir to combine.

3. Sift the flour and ginger together into a bowl.

4. Remove the pan containing the butter from the heat and cool slightly.

5. Fold the flour mixture and lemon juice and brandy, if using, into the pan. Allow to cool for 10 minutes.

6. Drop the mixture by a rounded teaspoon for the tubes or a rounded dessertspoon for the baskets onto the baking sheets, leaving about 4cm between each one.

7. Cook for about 8 minutes, or until they spread out and look 'lacy'.

8. Allow to cool for 3–4 minutes, then lift each one with a palette knife and use the handle of a wooden spoon to curve the biscuit round if you are making tubes. To make baskets, shape them around one end of a wooden rolling pin or a small orange. Fill with whipped cream or custard and fresh fruit to serve.

Ice-cream Tuiles

These are ideal partners for ice-cream, fools or custard-based desserts. Use within two days or they lose their crispness. Store in an airtight container.

Makes 16–18

80g caster sugar
80g butter
55g flour

1. Preheat the oven to 190°C/gas mark 5. Grease 2 baking sheets.

2. Cream the butter and sugar in a mixing bowl until light and fluffy. Sift in the flour and fold in well.

3. Put the mixture a teaspoon at a time onto the baking sheets, leaving about 3cm around each one. Press them down gently with a palette knife.

4. Bake for 5–6 minutes, or until they have just begun to go golden in colour around the edges. While still hot, curve them around a rolling pin and leave to go cold and firm up.

Variation
Make dessert cups to hold mousses and chocolate desserts: use slightly more mixture to make each, and when cooked, shape around the end of a rolling pin or a small orange.

Ginger Biscuits

These are deliciously crispy, and the crystallised ginger adds texture and taste. They should keep for up to a week in an airtight tin.

Makes 20–24

110g butter
110g golden caster sugar
1 level teaspoon
   ground ginger
2cm piece crystallised
   ginger, chopped
   very finely
80g plain flour
30g self-raising flour

1. Preheat the oven to 150°/gas mark 2.

2. Cream the butter and sugar in a mixing bowl until light and soft.

3. Add the ginger in both forms, then sift in the flours.

4. Mix everything together with a metal spoon. The dough should be fairly stiff. Bring it together with your hands.

5. Break off small pieces and roll them into a ball. Place on a baking sheet – no need to grease – about 2cm apart.

6. Bake for 35–40 minutes, or until they are golden and have spread out.

7. Allow to cool on the sheet for 20 minutes before transferring to a wire rack to cool completely.

BISCUITS
My Notes

8
Special Occasion Cakes

There are certain times in our lives when it is fun to bake a special cake: not just at Christmas, but when any get-together with friends and family calls for a delicious cake of some kind. In this chapter you will find both simple and more elaborate recipes for all types of occasions.

Basic Sponge

Sponge cakes are ideal as bases for birthday and other anniversary cakes. They can be made in many different shapes and sizes to suit. When cool, the cake can be sliced in half and filled as necessary. It can be iced (no need for marzipan) with any type of icing; see pages 8–12 for ideas. This sponge keeps well for at least seven days in an airtight container.

Makes 1 x 18cm square, 20cm round or a 20cm ring cake

Serves 10–12

250g butter
250g golden caster sugar
280g self-raising flour
3 eggs, beaten
½ teaspoon
   vanilla extract
80g ground almonds
2–3 tablespoons milk

1. Preheat the oven to 180°C/gas mark 4. Grease and line the square or round tins or grease and lightly flour the ring tin.

2. Cream the butter and sugar in a mixing bowl until light and fluffy.

3. Add a tablespoon of the flour and beat in the eggs and vanilla.

4. Fold in the rest of the flour and ground almonds. Stir in the milk.

5. Spoon the mixture into the prepared tin and smooth out the top with the back of the spoon. Make a well in the centre of the square- or round-shaped cake.

6. Bake for 30–35 minutes, or until well risen, springy and golden brown.

7. Cool for 10 minutes in the tin, then transfer to a wire rack and remove the paper after another 20 minutes.

Chocolate Gateau

Gateaux are always a welcome addition to a party or family dinner. They are usually layered and filled with cream or jam – or both in some cases. The secret is not to overfill them, because this spoils the look of the finished cake and makes it difficult to serve. Most are best kept in the fridge and eaten in a short space of time. This chocolate gateau is an easy but very impressive cake for birthdays and other get-togethers. You will need an electric mixer or electric hand mixer to do it justice. Keep it in the fridge and eat within two days.

Serves 10–12

150g self-raising flour
25g cocoa powder
150g golden caster sugar
2 eggs
200ml milk
150g butter, softened to
    room temperature
150g dark chocolate,
    broken into
    small pieces (or
    chocolate chips)

For the filling
80ml double cream
80ml mascarpone cheese

For the chocolate topping
100g dark chocolate,
    broken into
    small pieces
80g butter
1 tablespoon cocoa
    powder to dust the
    top, optional
Chocolate buttons to
    decorate, optional

1. Preheat the oven to 180°C/gas mark 4. Grease and line the bases of 2 x 18cm sandwich tins.

2. Sift the flour and cocoa in a mixing bowl into a mixing bowl. Stir in the sugar.

3. Beat the eggs and milk together and pour into the dry ingredients.

4. Using an electric mixer, start to whisk on the lowest speed. When all the dry ingredients are incorporated, add the butter. Switch to the highest setting and whisk for 2 minutes.

5. Stir in the chocolate.

6. Divide the mixture between the prepared tins and smooth out the tops, making a small well in the centre of each.

7. Bake for 15–20 minutes, or until springy to the touch.

8. Allow to cool in the tin for 5 minutes, then transfer to a wire rack.

9. When the cake is cool, make the filling: whisk the cream and mascarpone cheese together until just combined. Don't overwhisk or it will become too stiff.

10. Use the cream mixture to sandwich the cakes together.

11. Make the topping by melting the chocolate and butter in a heatproof bowl placed over a pan of simmering water. When melted, stir, then spread evenly over the top of the cake. If you wish, dust the top with cocoa – this gives the effect of a large chocolate truffle. Arrange the chocolate buttons on the top – use as many as you like. I place a few very large chocolate buttons in the centre.

Summer Fruit Gateau

Ideal cake for a summer party, this cake needs to be eaten within 36 hours and stored in the fridge.

Serves 8–10

120g butter
120g golden caster sugar
120g self-raising flour
2 eggs
½ teaspoon
vanilla extract
3 tablespoons milk

*For the filling
and topping*
280ml double cream
1 tablespoon icing sugar
Grated zest of 1 orange
and 2 tablespoons
of the juice
2–3 tablespoons
raspberry jam
80g fresh raspberries
80g flaked almonds
(toast the almonds in
the preheating oven
for 5–8 minutes
until golden for
added flavour)
200g fresh strawberries,
hulled and sliced

1. Preheat the oven to 170°C/gas mark 3. Grease and line the bases of 2 x 18cm sandwich tins.

2. Cream the butter and sugar in a mixing bowl until light and fluffy.

3. Add 1 tablespoon of the flour and beat in the eggs and vanilla. Sift in the rest of the flour and fold in. Stir in the milk.

4. Divide the mixture between the tins and bake for 20–25 minutes, or until well risen and springy to the touch.

5. Cool for 5 minutes in the tins, then transfer to a wire rack.

6. Make the filling by putting the cream into a bowl and sifting in the icing sugar, orange zest and juice. Whisk everything together until just stiff but spreadable.

7. Spread the jam on one half of the cake and spoon a third of the cream mixture over the jam. Press the raspberries into the cream. Place the second cake on top.

8. Smooth the rest of the cream over the top and sides of the cake.

9. Press the toasted almonds around the sides of the cake.

10. Put the strawberries on top, layering the slices evenly and thickly.

Mocha Gateau

An easy but impressive coffee-chocolate cake that will keep for two days in an airtight container in the fridge.

Serves 8–10

200g butter
200g golden caster sugar
180g self-raising flour
30g cocoa powder
½ teaspoon
   baking powder
4 eggs, beaten

For the filling
150g butter
100g icing sugar
1 dessertspoon coffee
   granules dissolved
   in 2 tablespoons
   boiling water
1 tablespoon Tia Maria

For the topping
200ml double cream
2 tablespoons icing sugar
1 teaspoon coffee
   granules mixed with
   3 teaspoons
   boiling water
1 tablespoon Tia Maria
Grated dark chocolate,
   for decoration

1. Preheat the oven to 180°C/gas mark 4. Grease and line the bases of 2 x 20cm sandwich tins.

2. Cream the butter and sugar in a mixing bowl until light and fluffy.

3. In a separate bowl, sift the flour, cocoa powder and baking powder together.

4. Add 1 tablespoon of the flour and gradually beat in the eggs, adding another tablespoon of flour if necessary.

5. Sift the rest of the flour again into the creamed mixture and fold in with a metal spoon.

6. Divide the mixture between the prepared tins and smooth out the top of each cake; make a small well in the centre of each.

7. Bake for 20–25 minutes, until well risen and springy. Allow to cool while you make the filling.

8. Cream the butter until soft and sift in the icing sugar. Beat well.

9. Add the coffee and Tia Maria and beat again. Use this to sandwich the cakes together.

10. Make the topping by whipping the cream until firm and mixing in the rest of the ingredients until thick.

11. Spread over the top of the cake and decorate with plenty of grated dark chocolate.

All-purpose Rich Fruit Cake

A cake for Christmas, birthdays, weddings or any other celebration. Make it in a square or circular tin but let it mature for at least four weeks before using. Grease and line the tin: once on the inside with baking paper and twice round the outside with brown paper to protect the cake from burning. The outer paper should rise about 4cm above the tin's rim. Cut a round of paper large enough to fit over the top just in case the cake starts to brown too much. For best results, measure out all of your ingredients first.

Makes 1 x 18cm square or 20cm round cake

220g plain flour
¼ teaspoon salt
1 teaspoon mixed spice
½ teaspoon
    grated nutmeg
½ teaspoon cinnamon
250g currants
300g sultanas
300g raisins
150g glacé cherries
50g candied mixed peel
50g flaked almonds
220g butter
220g soft brown sugar
1 tablespoon
    black treacle
Grated zest and
    juice of 1 lemon
Grated zest of
    1 orange
5 eggs
50ml brandy or rum,
    plus 50ml to feed
    the cake after
    baking, optional

1. Preheat the oven to 170°C/gas mark 3. Sift the flour, salt and spices together into a bowl.

2. Put the fruit and almonds into a bowl and sprinkle over 1 tablespoon of the flour mixture. Mix well so that the flour is evenly distributed.

3. In a large mixing bowl, cream the butter, sugar, treacle and fruit juices and zests until the mixture is fluffy. Add 2 tablespoons of the flour.

4. Beat the eggs, then gradually beat them into the creamed mixture. Fold in half of the fruit, then half of the flour. Repeat until everything is well mixed. Fold in the brandy or rum.

5. Put the mixture into the prepared tin, level out the top and make a well in the centre. Bake the cake in the centre of the oven for 45 minutes. Turn down the heat to 150°C/gas mark 2 and bake for 2½ hours. After about 1½ hours, cover the top with a disk of paper if it is browning too quickly. Test for doneness by pushing a skewer in the centre; if it comes out clean, it is baked, but if mixture clings to the skewer bake for 30 minutes more and test again.

6. Leave to cool in the tin for 30 minutes, then transfer to a wire rack, leaving the paper on. Allow to cool for 1 hour before removing the paper.

7. Skewer the cake all over to a depth of about 3cm. Drizzle with the brandy or rum and leave the alcohol to seep in deeply. Wrap it first in greaseproof paper, then in a layer of foil and place in an airtight container.

8. After at least 4 weeks, you can top it with marzipan and icing (see pages 11 and 9) or decorate it with fruit and nuts: melt 5 tablespoons of apricot jam in a pan with 1 tablespoon water. Pass through a sieve; brush the top of the cake with the syrup. Cover with rows of walnuts, almonds and glacé cherries. Brush the syrup glaze over the fruit and nuts carefully without disturbing the pattern.

Simnel Cake

This cake was traditionally baked for the end of the Lenten fast, so is associated with Easter celebrations. The name comes from the Latin *simila*, which translates as the 'best wheat flour'. It should keep two to three weeks in an airtight container.

Makes 1 x 18cm round cake

120g butter
120g soft brown sugar
150g plain flour
3 eggs, beaten
1 level teaspoon
    mixed spice
350g dried fruit, raisins,
    currants and sultanas
50g of either glacé
    cherries or mixed
    candied peel
Grated zest of 1 lemon
2 tablespoons apricot
    jam, mixed with
    1 dessertspoon
    water, warmed in
    a pan and sieved

For the almond paste
120g golden caster sugar
120g ground almonds
1 egg, beaten
½ teaspoon
    almond extract

1. First, make the almond paste: put the sugar and ground almonds into a mixing bowl and stir well. Add half of the egg and almond extract, and stir until the egg is combined with dry ingredients. Add more egg until the mixture is soft and pliable. Knead for a minute, then cover and put to one side for later.

2. Preheat the oven to 150°C/gas mark 2. Grease and line a deep 18cm round cake tin. Cream the butter and sugar in a mixing bowl until fluffy. Add a tablespoon of flour and beat in the eggs gradually.

3. Sift the flour and spice together, then gradually fold it into the creamed mixture. As you do so, add the fruit and lemon zest gradually until everything is incorporated. Spoon half the mixture into the prepared tin and smooth out the surface.

4. Divide the almond paste into 2 equal sections and roll 1 half to just fit the top of the cake mixture in the tin. Place it carefully on top.

5. Spoon the rest of the cake mixture over the top of the almond paste. Smooth the top and make a small well in the centre.

6. Turn the temperature of the oven down to 140°C/gas mark 1 and bake for 1½ hours. Test with a skewer to see if the cake is done; if necessary, bake for 30 minutes more.

7. Cool in the tin for 15 minutes, then transfer to a wire rack. Allow to cool with the paper on for 30 minutes before removing.

8. When the cake is completely cold, brush the top with the sieved apricot jam. Cut the rest of the almond paste in half and roll out one half to cover the top thinly. Use the rest to make 11 small balls. Use water to moisten the places where the balls will sit and press them down lightly.

9. Heat the oven to 180°C/gas mark 4. Put the cake on a baking sheet and return it to the oven for 10–12 minutes, or until the almond paste has browned.

Old English Christmas Cake

A very rich cake that is best prepared in late September. It is a traditional Victorian recipe and the fruit is soaked for three days before finally mixing it with the flour and other ingredients.

Makes 1 x 18cm round cake

500g mixed raisins, sultanas, mixed peel and currants
120ml cold tea
50ml brandy
30ml cream sherry
150g plain flour
1 teaspoon ground cinnamon
¼ teaspoon grated nutmeg
150g dark brown sugar
120g glacé cherries, chopped
150g butter, melted
Grated zest of 1 lemon and 1 orange
50g chopped almonds
3 eggs
1 tablespoon black treacle

1. Put the fruit into a large mixing bowl and add the tea, brandy and sherry. Stir well, cover and leave for 3 days. Stir each day to ensure that the fruit is evenly soaked.

2. Preheat the oven to 140°C/gas mark 1. Grease and line a 20cm round cake tin. Wrap two layers of brown paper around the outside of the tin.

3. Sieve the flour and spices together in a separate bowl. Stir in the sugar.

4. Stir the glacé cherries, melted butter, zest and almonds into the fruit mixture, then stir everything into the flour mixture.

5. Beat the eggs and treacle together. Add to the cake mixture and stir in well.

6. Spoon the mixture into the prepared tin and put on a baking sheet to protect the cake from burning underneath.

7. Bake for 2¾–3 hours, or until firm to the touch. Test the centre with a skewer to see if it is done. No mixture should be on the skewer when tested. Bake for a further 30 minutes if necessary.

8. Cool in the tin for 30 minutes, then transfer to a wire rack. Wrap in greaseproof paper and a layer of foil and store in an airtight container for 3 months before covering in marzipan and icing.

SPECIAL OCCASION CAKES
My Notes

9

Sweet and Savoury Scones

Scones are one of the easiest treats to make, and homemade ones taste much better than shop-bought – even though one of our local bakers makes a very delicious fruited scone and sells it with a tiny pots of clotted cream and preserves. The taste as they just begin to cool, the butter or cream melting down the sides and the whole messy business of eating them are what make them so special. There is nothing quite like them.

I remember many little villages we have visited by the kind of scones they have served. One of the best was on Anglesey, where they served homemade preserves and sold them in their shop next door.
There are many recipes for scones; some are sweet and fruited; some are plain; and my favourites are made with cheese and are *very* savoury. They are best eaten fresh on the day they are baked, but may be reheated in the oven for ten minutes the next day.

Even though they are very simple to make, following the tips below will ensure that you have successful scones every time.

1. Make sure your dough is soft, but not too sticky to handle.
2. Handle the mixture as little as possible.
3. Whisking the egg into the milk with a small whisk helps bring air into the scones and keep them light.
4. Bake straight away; any delay can cause a heavier scone.
5. Always preheat your oven – scones need a high temperature to rise.
6. Cool slightly before eating.

Basic Plain Scones

The following recipe is the classic plain scone that is usually served with preserves and cream. It uses lemon juice in order to acidify the milk. This makes the scone light, acting on the bicarbonate of soda in the baking powder. We don't like our scones too sweet, but if you prefer, add another half to one tablespoon of extra sugar.

I usually make scones with white flour, but you can use brown or wholemeal. If using only wholemeal, however, add a little more milk to the mixture and be prepared for a heavier scone. A combination of white and wholemeal flours works well, and the finished product has a light texture. Try different combinations; you will soon find which you prefer.

Makes 12–14

450g self-raising flour
1 teaspoon
    baking powder
1 level teaspoon salt
1 tablespoon golden
    caster sugar
55g butter, chopped
    into small pieces
1 tablespoon lemon juice
380ml milk

Variations
• For a wonderful flavour, use buttermilk or milk that is just beginning to sour in place of lemon juice and regular milk.

• Add 60g dried fruit just after rubbing in the butter. Chop larger dried fruit into bite-sized pieces before adding.

1. Preheat the oven to 220°C/gas mark 7. Grease 2 baking sheets.

2. Sift the flour, baking powder and salt together in a mixing bowl. Stir in the sugar.

3. Add the butter and rub it lightly into the flour with your fingertips until the mixture looks like fine breadcrumbs.

4. Add the lemon juice to the milk and stir vigorously until it thickens slightly. Mix this into the flour with a fork using light, quick strokes to form a soft, pliable dough. If it is too sticky the mixture will spread and the scones will be a funny shape, but a soft dough rises better and makes a lighter scone. Bring the dough together by kneading lightly.

5. Either form the dough into one large round with your hands and bake it, cutting it into wedges when cooked, or roll it out on a floured surface to about 2.5cm thick. Use either a fluted or plain cookie cutter and press straight down without twisting, (if you twist, your scone it won't rise as much). Each time you make another shape, dip your cutter into a little flour to make removing the cutter easier.

6. Put the scones on the baking sheets, brush the tops with a little milk and bake for 20 minutes until golden brown. Cool 10 minutes if eating them straight away; otherwise they are impossible to slice in half. If required, they will keep warm and soft wrapped in a tea towel for an hour or so.

7. Serve with cream and jam of your choice or just some butter. Delicious!

Rich Sultana Scones

Makes 8 large scones

250g self-raising flour
½ teaspoon
   baking powder
½ teaspoon salt
80g butter, cut
   into pieces
80g sultanas
30g golden caster sugar
1 egg
160ml milk or buttermilk

1. Preheat the oven to 225°C/gas mark 7. Grease 1 baking sheet.

2. Sift the flour, baking powder and salt into a mixing bowl. Rub in the butter and stir in the fruit and sugar.

3. Whisk the egg into the milk and add to flour mixture, stirring in quickly.

4. Bring the mixture together to form a soft dough. Roll out on a floured surface to about 2.5cm thick. Using either a fluted or plain cookie cutter, press straight down into the dough without twisting. Each time you make another shape, dip your cutter into a little flour.

5. Put the scones on the baking sheets and brush the tops with a little milk.

6. Bake for 15–20 minutes until golden brown. Cool for 10 minutes before eating.

Apricot and Raisin Scones

Makes 8 large scones

250g self-raising flour
½ teaspoon
   baking powder
½ teaspoon salt
55g butter, cut
   into pieces
40g chopped ready-to-
   eat apricots
25g raisins
30g sugar
1 egg
160ml milk or buttermilk

1. Preheat the oven to 220°C/gas mark 7. Grease 1 baking sheet.

2. Sift the flour, baking powder and salt into a mixing bowl. Rub in the butter and stir in the fruit and sugar.

3. Whisk the egg into the milk and add to the flour mixture, stirring in quickly.

4. Bring the mixture together to form a soft dough. Roll out on a floured surface to about 2.5cm thick. Using either a fluted or plain cookie cutter, press straight down into the dough without twisting. Each time you make another shape, dip your cutter into a little flour.

5. Put the scones on the baking sheets and brush the tops with a little milk.

6. Bake for 15–20 minutes until golden brown. Cool for 10 minutes before eating.

Blueberry and Cream Scones

These are slightly heavier in texture but they almost melt in the mouth. They do need to be eaten on the day of baking, so only make what you need. Wash the blueberries in very hot water and dry them well before using; this brings out the flavour prior to cooking.

Makes 6

180g self-raising flour
½ level teaspoon
   baking powder
60g butter, cut into
   small pieces
2 tablespoons golden
   caster sugar
80–100g blueberries,
   washed and dried
1 egg
120ml single cream
1 dessertspoon
   demerara sugar

1. Preheat the oven to 220°C/gas mark 7. Grease a baking sheet.

2. Sieve the flour and baking powder together.

3. Rub in the butter.

4. Stir in the sugar and the blueberries.

5. Beat the egg into the cream and mix well into the dry ingredients.

6. Form the dough into 1 large round or roll out on a floured surface to about 2.5cm thick and cut into individual rounds: using either a fluted or plain cookie cutter, press straight down into the dough without twisting, (if you twist your scone it won't rise as much). Each time you make another shape, dip your cutter into a little flour to make removing the cutter easier.

7. Put the scone(s) on the baking sheets and brush them with a little milk.

8. Sprinkle the top with the demerara sugar and bake for 15–20 minutes.

9. Cool for 10 minutes before eating.

Two-cherry Scones

Using two types of cherries in this recipe gives these scones an extra-special taste.

Makes 8 large scones

250g self-raising flour
½ level teaspoon
  baking powder
½ teaspoon salt
55g butter, cut into
  small pieces
40g glacé cherries,
  rinsed and halved
15g dried cherries
20g sugar
1 egg
180ml milk or buttermilk

1. Preheat oven to 225°C/gas mark 7. Grease 1 baking sheet.

2. Sift the flour, baking powder and salt into a mixing bowl.

3. Rub in the butter and stir in the fruit and sugar.

4. Whisk the egg into the milk and add this to the flour mixture, stirring in quickly.

5. Bring the mixture together to form a soft dough.

6. Roll out on a floured surface to about 2.5cm thick. Using either a fluted or plain cookie cutter, press straight down into the dough without twisting, (if you twist your scone it won't rise as much). Each time you make another shape, dip your cutter into a little flour to make removing the cutter easier.

7. Put the scones on the baking sheets and brush the tops with a little milk.

8. Bake for 15–20 minutes until golden brown. Cool for 10 minutes before eating.

Spicy Fruit and Oat Scones

Use runny natural yoghurt instead of milk to make these scones. It makes them very light and tasty.

Makes 1 large or 6–8 individual scones

200g self-raising flour
1 teaspoon
   baking powder
½ teaspoon
   ground cinnamon
A pinch grated nutmeg
50g butter
50g golden caster sugar
50g mixed dried fruit
100g porridge oats
1 egg, beaten
180ml runny
   natural yoghurt

1. Preheat the oven to 220°C/gas mark 7. Grease a baking sheet.

2. Sieve the flour, baking powder and spices into a large mixing bowl.

3. Rub in the butter and stir in the sugar, fruit and oats.

4. Beat the egg and yoghurt together and add to the dry ingredients. Stir with a metal spoon until it is all combined.

5. Bring the dough together with your hands and knead lightly.

6. Form the dough into a large round or roll out on a floured surface to about 2.5cm thick and cut into individual rounds: using either a fluted or plain cookie cutter, press straight down into the dough without twisting, (if you twist your scone it won't rise as much). Each time you make another shape, dip your cutter into a little flour to make removing the cutter easier.

7. Bake for 15–20 minutes until golden in colour.

8. Cool for 10 minutes before eating.

SAVOURY SCONES

Scones don't have to be sweet! Savoury ones are just as easy to make and are a tasty alternative to bread served with soup. Eat them at lunchtime or take them on picnics instead of lots of sandwiches. Savoury scones are traditionally formed in a round shape and cut into sections after baking, but as with the sweet scones, if you prefer, roll them out and cut into individual rounds.

Herb Scones

Make 8 large scones

250g self-raising flour
1 level teaspoon salt
½ teaspoon
   baking powder
1 level teaspoon mixed
   dried herbs
2 tablespoons
   grated Parmesan
Black pepper to taste
55g butter, cut into
   small pieces
1 egg
160ml milk
   or buttermilk

1. Preheat the oven to 220°C/gas mark 7. Grease 1 baking sheet.

2. Sift the flour, salt and baking powder into a mixing bowl.

3. Stir in the herbs, cheese and pepper, then mix well.

4. Rub in the butter. Beat the egg into the milk and add this to the dry ingredients.

5. Gently bring the mixture together with your hands until the dough is formed. Form it into a round shape, put it on the baking sheet and press down carefully to flatten the round. Alternatively, roll out on a floured surface to about 2.5cm thick. Using either a fluted or plain cookie cutter, press straight down into the dough without twisting, (if you twist your scone it won't rise as much). Each time you make another shape, dip your cutter into a little flour to make removing the cutter easier.

6. Bake in the oven for about 20–25 minutes until golden.

7. Allow to cool for a few minutes, then cut the round into 8 equal pieces.

Cheese Scones

These are my absolute favourite and can be made in a jiffy. These are best served hot with butter dripping out of them. Toast any leftovers the next day – they taste just as good. You don't need any extra butter in the preparation of these scones because the fat in the cheese is sufficient.

Makes 8 large scones

250g self-raising flour
½ teaspoon
   baking powder
I level teaspoon salt
Black pepper
½–I teaspoon
   dry mustard
120g mature Cheddar
   (or any strong
   cheese), grated
I egg
160ml milk or buttermilk

1. Preheat the oven to 220°C/gas mark 7. Grease 1 baking sheet.

2. Sift the flour, baking powder, salt, pepper and mustard powder together in a bowl and stir in three-quarters of the cheese.

3. Beat the egg and milk together and stir this into the dry ingredients.

4. Mix well with your hands, kneading lightly.

5. Form into a round on the baking sheet, flatten slightly and sprinkle the rest of the cheese on the top. Alternatively, roll out on a floured surface to about 2.5cm thick. Using either a fluted or plain cookie cutter, press straight down into the dough without twisting, (if you twist your scone it won't rise as much). Each time you make another shape, dip your cutter into a little flour to make removing the cutter easier. Sprinkle each scone with cheese.

6. Bake for 15–20 minutes until golden on the top and well risen.

Variations
Use other ingredients to vary the flavour, such as:

• 30g chopped sun-dried tomatoes and 2 tablespoons Parmesan

• 25g chopped black olives and 50g of cubed feta cheese

• 2 tablespoons chopped fresh parsley and 100g well-drained flaked tuna

• 1 level teaspoon paprika pepper and some chopped chorizo sausage

• Cut the cheese quantity to 80g, add 3 rashers of chopped crispy bacon and 50g grated smoked cheese

SWEET AND SAVOURY SCONES
My Notes

10
Meringues

During many years of baking I have had more disasters with meringues
than anything else. This has made me realise that there are some hard
and fast rules for their preparation – which is precisely why I am
going to pass these on to you.

Really, a meringue is simply whisked egg whites and sugar, but sometimes
other ingredients may be added to help stabilise the mixture. This means that
the whites will hold on to the air and sugar better and not begin to separate;
when the latter happens, you will see droplets of liquid on your meringue and
underneath it. Cornflour or cream of tartar can be used to stabilise meringues,
and these will be mentioned in a recipe if it is necessary.

HOW TO MAKE PERFECT MERINGUES

- Use eggs that are as fresh as possible. They retain air more successfully after whisking.

- Chill the eggs for 30 minutes to aid the separation of white from yolk. Then allow the whites to reach room temperature for 30 minutes before whisking.

- Use a metal pot or glass bowl to prepare your meringues; plastic ones harbour grease.

- To make sure the bowl and all utensils are completely grease-free, rub half a lemon over them after washing and pat dry with kitchen paper.

- Don't boil a kettle just before whisking the whites – the humidity will have an effect on them and moisten the finished meringue, making it soggy.

- The best ratio to use is one large egg white to 55g sugar.

- Always add the sugar gradually, as this will help the egg whites retain air. A tablespoon at a time is perfect.

- Always use caster or icing sugar – never granulated, which is too coarse. Some recipes call for a combination of caster and icing sugar.

- For a firm meringue, add the sugar when the whites have been whisked sufficiently to form stiff peaks; for softer meringues, add it when the whites form soft peaks. Soft peaks fall over slightly when left. Stiff peaks stand firm.

- When preparing egg whites, don't stop and do another job halfway through: this will allow the air to escape.

- A meringue has been whisked long enough when it becomes very glossy and stays on a spoon turned upside down.

- When ready to bake, use good-quality baking or silicone paper to line the baking sheets.

- Meringues are firmer and more crisp on the top when baked at a low temperature for a longer time. However, some recipes using meringue as a topping or covering require a high temperature just to colour it and set the outside.

- When serving meringue, use a damp, sharp knife to slice it. This will give a clean cut without breaking or crumbling.

Mini Meringues

These are delicious sandwiched together with cream and make a useful accompaniment for ice cream. Dip them in chocolate to decorate desserts.

Makes 18–20

2 large egg whites
110g caster sugar
1 level tablespoon
 cornflour, sifted
 before adding

1. Preheat the oven to 150°C/gas mark 2. Line 2 baking sheets with paper.

2. Whisk the egg whites until stiff peaks are formed.

3. Whisk in the sugar gradually.

4. Whisk in the cornflour until the mixture is glossy and firm.

5. Put teaspoonfuls of the meringue onto the baking sheets and shape them into little mounds.

6. Bake for 30 minutes, or until they are crisp and golden.

7. Allow to cool on the baking sheet.

Serving suggestions
• Whip 80ml double cream until firm (but not too stiff) and use it to sandwich two mini meringues together.

• Dip them in 100g melted chocolate (you can also use this to sandwich them together) to decorate a special cake or trifle.

• Simply serve them with your favourite ice cream, fool or bananas and custard – one of my favourites!

Strawberry Pavlova

This can be made with raspberries or blackberries, or a summer combination of various berry fruits. This dessert is best assembled just before serving (meringue doesn't chill well).

Serves 8

5 egg whites
100g caster sugar
75g icing sugar

For the filling
250g mascarpone cheese
50ml single cream
300g fresh
 strawberries, sliced
1 dessertspoon icing
 sugar

1. Preheat the oven to 150°C/gas mark 2.

2. Put the egg white in a bowl and whisk until it forms peaks; this should take about 3–4 minutes.

3. Add the sugar 2 tablespoons at a time and whisk in. Alternate between caster and icing sugar. When all the sugar is whisked in, the meringue should be glossy and firm.

4. Put a sheet of silicone or baking paper on a baking sheet; a little of the meringue mixture underneath will help keep it in place.

5. Using a metal tablespoon, spoon the mixture into a circle about 20cm in diameter. Put more spoonfuls around the edge of the circle to raise the sides.

6. Just before putting the meringue in the oven, turn the heat down to 140°C/gas mark 1. Bake for 1 hour, then turn off the heat, but leave the meringue to dry out in the cooling oven.

7. When the meringue is cool, whip the mascarpone and cream together and spoon this mixture over the centre of the meringue.

8. Arrange the fruit over the cheese mixture and dust the whole thing with the icing sugar just before serving.

MERINGUES
My Notes

11
Baking Bread

Baking bread of all kinds is a great pleasure, one that can really lift the spirits if you're feeling a bit blue or out of sorts. Compared to when I first started baking bread about 30 years ago, today's range of flours suitable for bread-making is, frankly, amazing, but don't let the vast amount of choice put you off. Finding the right flour for your basic bread really is easy. Even if a certain type of flour is expensive, this simply means that your own bread will cost about as much as buying a shop-bought loaf – yet it will be fresher and taste that much better. Over the years, I have used all kinds of flour to bake bread; however, I've found that inexpensive supermarket own brands are every bit as good as the more expensive ones.

What should you look for?

Wheat flour is the most suitable flour for bread-making, mainly because it has the right amount of gluten, tastes good and produces consistently good-quality bread. Other types of grain can also be made into flour, such as rye or oats, but these are not suitable for bread-making on their own because they make a very heavy loaf due to their low amounts of gluten.

The best texture and flavour of a loaf are achieved by preparing the dough with what is known as 'strong' flour. This has a very high gluten content – much higher than other flours – and it is this that makes the dough elastic and gives the loaf texture, substance and volume. So when purchasing flour, look on the pack for the words 'strong' and 'suitable for bread-making'. That said, ordinary plain flour will make a reasonably good loaf, but if used on its own, it mustn't be left to prove for long – it falls more easily because it doesn't have the same body. It also doesn't keep as well.

Types of bread flours

White is the easiest to use. It consists of milled grain with the bran and wheatgerm removed. Buy unbleached flour if, like me, you prefer creamy coloured bread to a stark-white loaf.

Wholemeal or wholewheat is exactly what it says: flour made using the whole grain. Nothing is removed and nothing added. Sometimes the package may state that barley or rye flour has been added, but this isn't necessary.

Brown flour contains ten to 15 percent less bran than wholemeal so it makes a lighter-textured loaf, but be warned: some 'brown' flours are simply white flours with caramel added, so they don't benefit from the remaining whole grains. The packet should state what is actually in the flour.

Granary has malted wheat or barley added to the wholemeal to give it that characteristic nutty and slightly sweet flavour. This is because the added grains have been allowed to germinate slightly and unleash some of the sugars from the germ.

Rye This grain gives a denser and crumblier texture to bread and is the main ingredient in German pumpernickel. It is very low in gluten, so the bread doesn't rise, but instead has a dense texture. It can have a bitter taste so should be used in moderation at first until you're sure whether or not you like it.

Oats Oats have a low gluten content so are usually added to wheat flour. But oats are one of my favourite bread ingredients because they provide flavour, texture and the extra nutritional benefits associated with them.

Cornmeal or maize is mixed with wheat flour and makes wonderful cornbread.

Rice is usually added to wheat flour, or used in unleavened bread.

Soya is used to enrich the protein content of bread. Use too much, however, and the bread may become heavy.

Chickpea or gram flour is used to make chapattis and unleavened breads. It is also used to make meat and vegetable pakoras.

What makes bread rise?

The leavening or raising agent in most bread is yeast. Soda is another popular leavening ingredient.

Yeast causes bread to rise by producing carbon dioxide, and it is this that is released into the dough during proving, causing it to swell and stretch.

Yeast is a living organism that requires certain conditions in order to function as a raising agent. When purchased, it is dormant and needs reactivating before use. To do this, the yeast must have heat, food and liquid. Too much heat will kill it, however, so a lukewarm liquid is generally added to the yeast or flour, along with a small amount of sugar to serve as its food. Water or milk are used as the liquid. Either fresh or dried yeast may also be used to make bread, but dried is easier to come by. There are three kinds of dried yeast:

Standard dried yeast is granulated and comes in small tins. This type needs reconstituting before use.

Easy-blend dried yeast consists of fine granules that may be added straight to the flour without reconstituting. It is bought in sachets or small drums.

Fast-action easy-blend dried yeast is granular and purchased in sachets; it is mixed in with the flour and contains ascorbic acid or vitamin C. This is added to speed up the yeast's action on the dough, and using it speeds up the rising process so that only one proving time is necessary. This is the yeast I use for everyday bread-making.

Soda Bread made without yeast tends to use soda as its raising agent, in the same way as cakes. Soda bread is prepared very quickly and can be made with plain or strong flour.

What are the basic processes in baking bread?

This depends on the type of yeast you are using, because fresh and some dried yeast needs reactivating, as mentioned above. This will be explained in the recipes that use this process. If using fresh or ordinary dried yeast, the basic steps in making bread are as follows.

Mixing involves preparing the dough using flour, yeast, liquid, salt and any other ingredients the recipe calls for. Always mix the salt in *before* the yeast; never add them together or the salt will kill the yeast.

Kneading is the pummelling action that is necessary to stretch and break down the gluten in the flour. If making a small amount of dough, I tend to do this in the mixing bowl as it keeps the dough warm and gives it a good shape. Hold the dough in one hand and pull at it with the other. Allow it to stretch, then fold it back over and pull out another bit. Repeat this for about 10 minutes. The dough should be smooth with an elastic texture when sufficiently kneaded. Prod it with your finger and the dimple should recover quickly. Thorough kneading makes a soft, good-textured finished bread.

Proving is when the dough is left to rise. The yeast will be doing its job and producing carbon dioxide, which causes the dough to expand and gain size. This is essential for a light-textured bread.

Knocking back gets rid of any large air pockets that may cause an uneven dough. Grab the bread and punch it down, then knead for 1–2 minutes to allow it to regain an even texture.

Shaping is when you shape the bread into whatever you wish. Round or oval cobs, plaits and small rolls are the most popular and easiest to do. This is a matter of preference. Use oiled tins or baking sheets. If using a tin, simply shape the dough to the required tin. Allow for a doubling in size, however, so make sure the tin is large enough to accommodate the bread.

Second proving This is when the shaped dough is left in a warmish place and allowed to double in size again. Depending on the type of yeast used (see previous page), you may not need this step.

Finishing is what you do to the crust just before baking. You can finish the top with seeds, oats or other ingredients as stated in the recipe. The crust can also be brushed with egg and milk for a shine, or with vegetable oil for a crispy crust.

Baking kills the yeast – and obviously cooks the dough. Most bread is baked at a high temperature, but some recipes ask for this to be reduced during baking time so that the bread doesn't bake too quickly on the outside while the inside remains doughy and slightly raw. This can happen if baking a large loaf. Because it is impossible to say exactly how long a loaf should bake as this depends on your oven and the final size of the bread, it is important to know how to check if a loaf is done. There are two ways to do this: by the appearance and sound of the loaf. If the loaf is baked in a tin, it should be slightly shrunken away from the sides, and the crust should be deep golden and firm to the touch. To hear whether it's done, use oven gloves to lift out the loaf and tap it underneath – you should hear a hollow, resonant sound. If not, then leave the dough to cook for 10 more minutes on a slightly lower heat.

Cooling This is important, because if you slice a loaf too soon, you squash it and it will never recover its shape. Leave at least 30 minutes for a large loaf and 15 for small loaves or individual rolls.

Standard White Loaf

This bread is made using fresh or ordinary dried yeast. You can use it to make 12–15 individual rolls, or a combination of eight to ten rolls plus one larger loaf. You can make it using brown or wholemeal flour instead of white, or half white and half wholemeal. You may need a little more water with wholemeal flour because it absorbs more liquid than white.

Makes 4 small or 3 medium-sized loaves

25g fresh yeast or
  15g dried yeast
½ teaspoon sugar
750–900ml warm water
1kg strong white flour
3 teaspoons salt
2–3 tablespoons
  vegetable or
  sunflower oil

1. Crumble or pour the yeast into a small jug. Add the sugar and about 4–5 tablespoons of the warm water. Stir and put in a warm place.

2. Mix the flour and salt together in a large mixing bowl and make a well in the centre. Pour in the yeast mixture, and add the oil and half of the rest of the water. Sprinkle over some of the flour to seal in the heat and leave for 15 minutes in a warm place. The mixture should be frothy in the centre.

3. Use a wooden spoon to mix the liquid into the dough. Now use your hands to mix in as much of the warm water as necessary to make a soft dough that is easy to handle. Remember that a moist dough makes a softer bread, so don't worry if it is sticky at first; as you knead it you can add a little more flour and it will become smoother and less sticky.

4. Start kneading the dough in the bowl. If you find it easier, however, dust a clean work surface with flour and knead for 10–15 minutes.

5. Put the dough back into the bowl if necessary, cover it with a tea towel and leave to prove for about 1–1½ hours in a warm place, or until it has doubled in size.

6. Put the dough onto a lightly floured surface and divide it into 3 or 4 portions. Knead for 2–3 minutes and shape as desired.

7. Place on an oiled baking sheet or oiled tins. Leave to prove again for about 40 minutes. Don't overprove it or it will lose its shape and texture. When it is ready it will be puffy and light to touch.

8. About 10 minutes before baking, preheat the oven to 220°C/gas mark 7.

9. Bake the bread for 25 minutes, then turn the loaves around and reduce the heat to 200°C/gas mark 6. Bake for 10–15 more minutes, or until done.

10. Remove from the tins or from the baking sheets immediately and allow to cool on a wire rack.

Simple White Bread

This is the recipe I use most of the time and it can be made from brown, wholemeal or a combination of flours. Remember to add a little more liquid if using all wholemeal flour.

Makes 2–3 medium-sized loaves

1kg strong white flour
2 level teaspoons salt
2 x 7g sachets fast-action dried yeast
750–900ml warm water
2 tablespoons oil (vegetable, sunflower or olive)

1. Sieve the flour and salt together into a large mixing bowl. If you are using wholemeal or brown flour, then simply pour into the bowl and stir in the salt.

2. Stir in the yeast.

3. Make a well in the centre of the flour and pour in half of the water and all the oil.

4. Stir together first with a wooden spoon, then use your hands to combine, adding more water until the dough is moist and soft and all the flour is combined.

5. Begin kneading the dough in the bowl, dusting it with a little flour to make it more easy to handle if necessary.

6. Finish on a work surface if you find it easier. Continue kneading for 10 minutes.

7. Divide the dough as you wish and shape it as desired. Place in lightly oiled tins or on baking trays, cover and leave to prove in a warmish place until doubled in size: about 40–45 minutes.

8. After about 30 minutes of proving, preheat the oven to 220°C/gas mark 7.

9. Bake the bread for 20 minutes, then turn the tin or tray around and reduce the heat to 200°C/gas mark 6. Bake for 8–10 more minutes, or until done.

10. Remove from the tin and cool on a wire rack.

Oatmeal Loaf

Makes 2 medium-sized loaves

500g strong brown,
  wholemeal or
  white flour
200g fine oatmeal
2 teaspoon salt
2 x 7g sachets
  fast-action yeast
580–650ml warm water
2 tablespoons oil

1. In a large mixing bowl stir the flour, oatmeal and salt together well. Stir in the yeast.

2. Make a well in the centre and add half of the water and all the oil.

3. Stir together with a wooden spoon, then use your hands. Add enough of the remaining water to make a soft, moist dough.

4. Start to knead the dough, dusting with more flour if necessary to make it easier to handle.

5. Knead it in or out of the bowl for 10 minutes.

6. Divide the dough as necessary and form into loaves.

7. Place on oiled baking sheets, cover and leave to prove for 35–45 minutes in a warmish place, until doubled in size.

8. Preheat the oven to 220°C/gas mark 7 and bake for 20 minutes, then turn the loaves and bake for a further 5–10 minutes.

9. Allow to cool on a wire rack.

Milk Loaf

This makes a very soft bread – and amazingly crispy toast.

Makes 1 large loaf

400g strong white flour
1 level teaspoon salt
1 tablespoon dried milk
1 x 7g sachet fast-action
 dried yeast
250–280ml whole
 milk, warmed

1. Put the flour in a large mixing bowl, and stir or sieve in the salt and dried milk.

2. Stir in the yeast.

3. Pour the warm milk over the flour and stir in well with a wooden spoon.

4. Use your hands to bring the dough together and knead in the bowl, adding more flour if necessary.

5. Continue kneading for 10 minutes.

6. Shape into a long oval and place on a lightly oiled baking sheet.

7. Cover with a tea towel and leave to prove in a warm place for 40–45 minutes, or until doubled in size.

8. Preheat the oven to 220°C/gas mark 7.

9. Bake for 20 minutes, then turn down the heat to 190°C/gas mark 5 and bake for 15–20 minutes more, or until baked.

Herb Bread

This bread is soft, with an open texture, and is ideal served with pâté, soup or salads.

Makes 1 loaf or 2 small loaves

350g strong white flour
1 teaspoon salt
1 x 7 g sachet fast-action dried yeast
2 tablespoons finely chopped fresh mixed herbs (or 1½ level teaspoons dried)
200ml warm milk
1 egg, beaten
1 tablespoon oil
1 teaspoon poppy seeds

1. Put the flour in a bowl and stir in the salt, then the yeast.

2. Stir in the herbs.

3. Mix the milk and egg in a jug and stir.

4. Make a well in the centre of the flour and pour in the egg and milk mixture, but reserve a tablespoons to brush the top of the loaf. Add the oil.

5. Stir well with a wooden spoon and knead together with your hands. If the mixture is too sticky, add a little more flour and work it in.

6. Knead the dough for 10 minutes.

7. Oil a loaf tin or 2 small tins.

8. Divide the dough if necessary and shape it to fits the tin(s) lengthways.

9. Cover the tins with a tea towel and leave to prove in a warmish place for 45 minutes. Brush the tops with the reserved egg/milk mixture and sprinkle with the poppy seeds.

10. Preheat the oven to 220°C/gas mark 7.

11. Bake for 20 minutes, then turn the heat down to 200°C/gas mark 6 and bake for a further 12 minutes for 2 small loaves or 15–20 minutes for a large one.

12. Remove from the tins and allow to cool on a wire rack.

Onion Bread

This is delicious with soups. We also have it with curries in place of rice.

Makes 1 large, flat loaf

450g strong white flour
2 teaspoons salt
1 x 7g sachet of fast-
    action dried yeast
½ teaspoon dried thyme
1 teaspoon onion seeds
270–300ml warm water
1 tablespoon oil

For the topping
1 dessertspoon oil,
    for frying
1 medium onion,
    finely chopped
1 clove garlic, crushed
1 level tablespoon
    plain flour
120ml milk
Salt and black pepper
    to taste
Onion seeds,
    to sprinkle on top

1. Sieve the flour and salt together into a bowl. Stir in the yeast, thyme and onion seeds.

2. Stir in the water and oil and bring everything together with your hands to form a dough.

3. Knead for 10 minutes.

4. Flatten into a large round and place the dough on a lightly oiled baking sheet. Leave to prove for 40–45 minutes.

5. Meanwhile, make the topping. Heat the oil in a frying pan and fry the onion and garlic over a gentle heat until they begin to caramelise. Sprinkle in the flour, stirring well. Gradually add the milk and stir until it thickens, keeping the heat low so that nothing burns. Season with salt and pepper and continue cooking for 2–3 minutes, stirring continuously. Remove from the heat and cool for 10 minutes.

6. Preheat the oven to 220°C/gas mark 7.

7. When the dough has finished proving, gently flatten it with just your fingertips and spread the onion mixture over the top.

8. Sprinkle with the onion seeds and bake for 10 minutes, then turn down the heat to 200°C/gas mark 6 for another 20–25 minutes.

9. Allow to cool on a rack for 20 minutes before serving.

Individual Rolls

These are great for parties or serving with soups and starter courses for a special dinner.

Makes between 15–20

800g strong white flour
2 level teaspoons salt
1x 7g sachet fast-action
  dried yeast
200ml warm milk
250ml warm water
1 tablespoon sunflower
  or rapeseed oil

1. Sieve the flour and salt together in a bowl. Stir in the yeast.

2. Combine the milk and water and pour into the flour with the oil.

3. Stir with a wooden spoon to combine all the ingredients and finish mixing the dough together with your hands.

4. Knead the dough for 10 minutes on a floured surface.

5. Shape into your desired shapes and sizes of rolls and place on a greased baking sheet. If you want to make sandwich or burger buns, roll the dough into small balls, then press them flat on the baking sheet.

6. Leave to prove in a warm place until doubled in size – about 30 minutes.

7. Preheat the oven to 220°C/gas mark 7.

8. For a professional finish, brush with a mixture of egg and milk: 1 beaten egg to 4 tablespoons milk. You could also sprinkle the tops with sesame or poppy seeds.

9. Bake for 15–20 minutes, then transfer to a rack to cool.

Soda Bread

Soda bread is made without using yeast; the leavening ingredient is a combination of baking powder and either buttermilk or milk with a tablespoon of lemon juice mixed in. This is a useful recipe that can be made with ordinary plain white flour if necessary. It is a quick and easy choice for times when you need bread fast. Soda bread doesn't keep for long and is best eaten within 24 hours, but it may be reheated or toasted to freshen it up.

Makes 1 large round loaf

250g strong white flour
1 level teaspoon salt
1 rounded teaspoon
   baking powder
200g strong
   wholemeal flour
280ml carton of
   buttermilk
   (or 280ml milk with
   1 tablespoon lemon
   juice added)

1. Preheat the oven to 220°C/gas mark 7. Grease a baking tray.

2. Sieve the white flour, salt and baking powder together into a bowl.

3. Stir in the wholemeal flour until it is combined with the other ingredients.

4. Add the milk or buttermilk and stir in. The mixture should be slightly sticky.

5. Bind with the hands but don't knead the dough. Form into a round.

6. Place the round on the prepared baking sheet and flatten it slightly. Use a sharp knife to cut a cross into the dough, about 2cm deep. This makes 4 sections.

7. Bake for 20–25 minutes until well risen and golden brown.

8. Cool for 10 minutes before serving.

Variation
Add a healthy dose of oats to your bread by substituting 100g medium rolled oats for 100g wholemeal or white flour. Add this to the mixture when you stir in the wholemeal flour, then follow the rest of the recipe.

Grandma's Rye Bread

This is a nutty-flavoured bread that really is very filling. I use ordinary dried yeast for this recipe as it needs to prove; otherwise it becomes too heavy.

Makes 2 medium loaves

15g ordinary dried yeast
½ teaspoon sugar
450–500ml warm water,
300g rye flour
250g strong white flour
250g fine oatmeal
3 teaspoons salt

1. Put the yeast into a jug with the sugar. Add 2–3 tablespoons of the warm water, stir and put to one side.

2. Mix all the dry ingredients together in a large bowl and stir well.

3. Make a well in the centre and pour in the yeast mixture and the rest of the warm water.

4. Stir everything together, then knead the mixture into a dough with your hands. If it is too dry, add a little extra warm water; if it is too sticky, add a little more strong white flour.

5. Knead on a floured work surface for 15–20 minutes.

6. Put the dough back into the bowl, cover and leave to prove for 35–40 minutes in a warm place, or until doubled in size.

7. Knock back and knead for 2–3 minutes, then divide the dough in half and form it into 2 oval loaves.

8. Place on a lightly oiled baking sheet and leave to prove for 30 minutes in a warm place. Preheat the oven to 200°C/gas mark 6.

9. Bake for 25–30 minutes, or until done.

10. Cool completely before serving.

Cornbread

This is a classic yet basic cornbread to which you may add your own ingredients, varying the flavour according to whatever you serve with it. Like soda bread, this does not call for yeast as a raising agent, but in this instance baking soda is used.

Makes 1 loaf

100g butter
1 level tablespoon sugar
2 eggs, beaten
230ml buttermilk or
　whole milk
130g plain white flour
1 teaspoon salt
1 rounded teaspoon
　baking soda
150g cornmeal

1. Preheat the oven to 180°C/gas mark 4. Lightly grease a 20cm square cake tin.

2. Put the butter and sugar in a pan and melt gently over a low heat. Remove from the heat as soon as the butter has melted.

3. Beat in the eggs and stir in the milk.

4. Sieve the flour, salt and baking soda together into a bowl. Stir in the cornmeal.

5. Make a well in the centre and pour in the butter mixture. Stir well with a wooden spoon until smooth.

6. Pour the batter into the prepared tin and bake for 30–40 minutes, or until well risen and springy to the touch.

Variations
• For a sweet version add 2 tablespoons of sugar and 80g raisins or sultanas to the flour mixture before adding the buttery liquid.

• To spice it up, add a teaspoon of ground cinnamon and a touch of nutmeg to the sifted flour.

Pumpernickel

This bread needs to mature for two days before eating, so be sure to make it in advance. Dark rye bread keeps well and is ideal to serve with cold meats and pickles, salads and sliced tomatoes.

Makes 2 loaves

25g dried yeast
750ml warm water
300g rye flour
650g wholemeal flour
2 teaspoons salt
1 tablespoon treacle

1. Mix the dried yeast with 3 tablespoons of the warm water and stir. Leave in a warm place.

2. Stir the flours together in a large mixing bowl, then stir in the salt.

3. Make a well in the flour and pour in the yeast mixture, half of the rest of the water and all the treacle.

4. Stir into the flour before stirring in the rest of the liquid.

5. Bring the dough together with your hands until smooth, then knead it for 15 minutes.

6. Leave to prove for 30 minutes, or until doubled in size. Knead again for 2–3 minutes.

7. Oil 2 loaf tins. Divide the dough into 2 equal sections and shape them to fit the tins. Leave to prove until the dough has doubled in size.

8. Preheat the oven to 200°C/gas mark 6.

9. Bake the loaves for 20 minutes, then turn the heat down to 190°C/gas mark 5 and bake for a further 25–30 minutes.

10. Remove from the tins and allow to cool completely before wrapping in greaseproof paper. Store in an airtight container for 48 hours before eating.

Focaccia

This is a simple version of the Italian bread and can be served with soups and main dishes. My favourite way is to serve it with mussels cooked in a light tomato and garlic sauce.

Makes 1 large loaf

450g strong white flour
1 level teaspoon salt
1 x 7g sachet
    fast-action yeast
250–300ml warm water
2 tablespoons olive oil
2 teaspoons coarse sea
    salt, for sprinkling

1. Put the flour and salt into a bowl and stir well. Stir in the yeast.

2. Make a well in the centre and add the water and oil. Stir to combine using a wooden spoon.

3. Use your hands to knead the dough until smooth, then knead for 10 minutes.

4. Leave to prove for 20 minutes in a warm place. Knead for 2 minutes, then leave to prove again for 30 minutes.

5. Lightly oil a baking tray. Work the dough into a flat, round shape about 3cm thick. Place on the prepared tray and press your fingertips deep into the dough to form indentations.

6. Preheat the oven to 220°C/gas mark 7.

7. Sprinkle the dough lightly with the sea salt, then bake for 25–30 minutes, or until a deep golden brown.

Variations
• Top with herbs and garlic instead of sea salt or grated Parmesan and black pepper.

• Add 15 chopped black olives to the dough while you knead it.

• Add 50g chopped sun-dried tomatoes, well-drained of oil.

French Stick

It is difficult to achieve the authentic taste and texture of real French baguettes without using French flour, but this is a wonderful substitute reminiscent of the fresh bread bought early on a sunny French morning.

Makes 3 baguettes

450g strong white flour
1 teaspoon salt
1 x 7g sachet
   fast-action yeast
300ml warm water
Beaten egg to glaze

1. Sieve the flour and salt together into a large mixing bowl. Stir in the yeast.

2. Mix in the warm water and knead the mixture together with your hands into a dough.

3. Knead for 10 minutes.

4. Leave for 20 minutes, then knead for 5 minutes. Lightly oil your longest baking sheet.

5. Divide into 3 equal portions. Stretch the dough lengthways and fold it over several times, stretching in the same direction each time. Do this with each portion of dough, then form them into long, thin, sausage shapes that will fit on your baking sheet.

6. Leave to prove for 30 minutes in a warm place.

7. Preheat the oven to 220°C/gas mark 7.

8. Brush the baguettes with the beaten egg and bake for 15–20 minutes.

Naan

Although this is traditionally made in a tandoori oven at high temperatures, you can make it in an ordinary oven so long as it is preheated for 10 minutes at its highest setting.

Makes 3

225g strong white flour
½ teaspoon salt
1 sachet fast-action yeast
4 tablespoons
  warm milk
1 tablespoon
  sunflower oil
2 tablespoons
  plain yoghurt
1 egg, beaten

1. Sieve the flour and salt together in a bowl. Stir in the yeast.

2. Mix in the other ingredients and bring the mixture together with your hands to form a dough.

3. Knead for 5 minutes, then leave in a warm place to double in size. This will take about 30–40 minutes.

4. Preheat the oven to its highest temperature. Heat some oil on a baking tray for 5 minutes.

5. Divide the dough into 3 pieces and roll each piece out into a teardrop shape.

6. Remove the baking tray from the oven and lay each naan on the hot tray. Bake immediately for 4–5 minutes until they have ballooned and started to turn golden brown.

7. Serve warm.

BAKING BREAD
My Notes

12
Sweet and Tea Breads

The smell of a spicy, sweet teacake or fruit loaf cooking is one of the most comforting scents that can fill a house, especially on a cold day. Sweetened dough keeps well after baking because it often contains a higher proportion of fat and, often, sugar, both of which are preservatives. Sweet and tea breads are often glazed with beaten egg and milk just before baking to give them a shiny, crisp crust.

Fruit Teacakes

If you prefer a plain teacake, simply omit the fruit. Try adding a level teaspoon of mixed spice to the flour and salt at the beginning of the recipe for a spicier flavour.

Makes 10–12

450g strong white flour
1 level teaspoon salt
1 x 7g sachet fast-action
   dried yeast
50g caster sugar
40g softened butter
300ml warm milk
50g currants
50g sultanas
25g mixed peel

1. Sieve the flour and salt into a mixing bowl. Stir in the yeast and sugar. Rub in the butter.

2. Make a well in the centre and pour in the milk. Stir, then mix with your hands to combine.

3. Knead to form a dough and then add the fruit and peel. Knead this all in and continue to knead for 3–4 minutes.

4. Break off equal amounts of the dough, roll into balls and place on a lightly oiled baking sheet. Press down into flat discs. Leave to prove for 30 minutes.

5. Preheat the oven to 220°C/gas mark 7.

6. Bake for 10–15 minutes, then cool on a wire rack before serving.

Sally Lunn

This rich bread was first made by Sally Lunn, who lived in Bath. She owned a celebrated baker's shop in Lilliput Alley – and her shop is still there today.

Makes 3 small loaves

380g strong white flour
½ teaspoon salt
1 x 7g sachet fast-action
   dried yeast
40g caster sugar
1 large egg, beaten
Finely grated rind
   of a lemon
150ml warm water
50g butter, melted gently
   over a low heat

1. Sieve the flour and salt together. Stir in the yeast and sugar.

2. Make a well in the centre of the dry ingredients and add the egg and lemon rind. Stir well. Stir in the water and mix thoroughly, then pour in the melted butter and mix in.

3. Knead the dough until smooth, then transfer to a lightly floured surface.

4. Divide the mixture into 3 sections and knead each for 3–4 minutes.

5. Place on an oiled baking sheet and leave to prove for 30 minutes in a warm place. Preheat the oven to 220°C/gas mark 7.

6. Just before baking, brush the tops with a little beaten egg. Bake for 15–20 minutes. Allow to cool completely before slicing.

Walnut Loaf

A delicious, nutty, fruity tea loaf that is wonderful toasted and spread with butter.

Makes 1 large loaf

450g strong white flour
1 teaspoon salt
1 x 7g sachet fast-action
    dried yeast
50g soft brown sugar
50g butter
300ml milk
100g raisins
50g sultanas
50g chopped apricots
80g chopped walnuts
Egg and milk to
    glaze, optional

1. Sieve the flour and salt together into a large mixing bowl. Stir in the yeast and sugar.

2. Put the butter and milk into a small pan over a low heat and allow the butter to melt into the milk.

3. Meanwhile, stir the fruit into the dry ingredients.

4. When the milk is warm and the butter has melted, make a well in the flour mixture and pour in the milk. Stir to combine thoroughly with a wooden spoon.

5. Use your hands to knead the dough for 10 minutes.

6. Grease a loaf tin large enough to take the dough when it has doubled in size. Place the dough in the tin, cover with a tea towel and leave it to prove in a warm place until doubled in size.

7. Preheat the oven to 220°C/gas mark 7.

8. Glaze with beaten egg and milk if desired and bake for 20 minutes, then turn down the heat to 190°C/gas mark 5 and bake for 10–15 more minutes, or until done.

9. Remove from the tin and allow to cool completely before slicing.

Chocolate Bread

An unusual loaf for chocolate-lovers.

Makes 1 loaf

400g strong white flour
1 teaspoon salt
30g cocoa powder (or
    50g for a strong
    chocolate flavour)
1 x 7g sachet fast-action
    dried yeast
50g soft brown sugar
50g butter, melted
280ml warm milk
100g dark chocolate,
    broken into
    small pieces

1. Sieve the flour, salt and cocoa together into a large mixing bowl.

2. Stir in the yeast and then the sugar.

3. Make a well in the centre of the dry ingredients and pour in the warm milk and butter. Stir with a wooden spoon until everything is combined.

4. Knead the dough for 10 minutes.

5. Flatten out the dough and add half of the chocolate, then fold up the dough and flatten again. Add the rest of the chocolate and fold, then gently knead in.

6. Place the dough in a greased loaf tin large enough to hold it once it has doubled in size. Leave to prove for 30–40 minutes, or until doubled.

7. Preheat the oven to 220°C/gas mark 7.

8. Bake for 20 minutes, then turn down the heat to 190°C/gas mark 5 for 10–15 minutes, or until done.

9. Remove the bread from the tin and allow to cool completely before serving.

Spicy Fruit Tea Loaf

This makes a great afternoon treat with tea or coffee or toasted for breakfast.

Makes 1 medium-sized loaf

500g strong white flour
1 teaspoon mixed spice
½ teaspoon
   ground cinnamon
1 level teaspoon salt
1 x 7g sachet fast-action
   dried yeast
50g golden caster sugar
50g softened butter
350ml warm milk
1 egg, beaten
50g currants
50g sultanas
25g mixed candied peel,
   optional; you can also
   use extra sultanas
   or currants

1. Sieve the flour, spices and salt together. Stir in the yeast and sugar.

2. Rub in the butter.

3. Combine the milk and the egg and pour gradually into the flour mixture, stirring well with a wooden spoon.

4. Begin to knead the dough and gradually knead in the dried fruit.

5. When the fruit is fully combined, knead the dough for 8–10 minutes, adding a little more flour if the mixture is too sticky.

6. Grease a loaf tin. Knead the dough into an oblong shape and place it in the prepared tin.

7. During the proving time, preheat the oven to 220°C/gas mark 7.

8. When the dough has doubled in size, bake for 20 minutes, turn the heat down to 200°C/gas mark 6 and bake for 5–10 minutes longer, or until fully baked. The loaves should be deep golden when done.

9. Leave to cool on a rack for at least 30 minutes before slicing.

Variation
To make individual teacakes, roll out the dough into 10 balls, put them on a greased baking sheet and flatten with your hand. Leave to prove in a warm place for 35 minutes and bake for 20–25 minutes. Leave the heat at 220°C/gas mark 7 for the whole of the baking time.

Mincemeat Chelsea Buns

If you have half a jar of mincemeat left over in your cupboard, don't make any more pies; try this recipe instead. These buns are delicious served hot or cold.

Makes about 8–10

1 teaspoon dried yeast
½ teaspoon sugar
120ml warm milk
300g strong flour
½ teaspoon salt
30g butter, melted
1 egg, beaten
About 5 tablespoons
   mincemeat
2 tablespoons
   clear honey

1. Mix the dried yeast with the sugar and warm milk. Leave in a warm place to froth up; this should take about 10–15 minutes.

2. Sieve the flour and salt together into a mixing bowl. Stir in the yeast mixture, melted butter and beaten egg. Stir everything together well.

3. Use your hands to knead the mixture, adding a dusting of flour if it becomes too sticky. Carry on kneading for 10 minutes until the dough is smooth.

4. Cover the dough and allow to prove for 30–40 minutes until doubled in size.

5. Flour a work surface and roll the dough out to a rectangle measuring about 34cm x 26cm.

6. Spread the mincemeat evenly over the surface of the dough.

7. Start with the longest edge and roll up the dough carefully into a long sausage shape with the open edge underneath.

8. Preheat the oven to 220°C/gas mark 7. Grease a baking sheet.

9. Cut the roll into 8–10 slices and lay them flat onto the baking sheet, close together.

10. Leave to prove for 20–30 minutes.

11. Bake for 20–25 minutes or until golden brown. Brush the tops of the hot buns with honey before serving.

Cinnamon Brioche

This is a classic French-style brioche flavoured with cinnamon and nutmeg. It can be baked in a 22cm x 13cm loaf tin or a traditional brioche mould. For a successful brioche, long, slow proving gives the best result, so leaving it to prove overnight in a fridge is ideal. The mixture is best prepared in a food processor, but a hand mixer with dough hooks will do.

Makes 1 loaf

1 tablespoon
   caster sugar
3 tablespoons hot water
1 x 7g sachet ordinary
   dried yeast
   (not fast-action)
150g plain
   (not strong) flour
1 teaspoon
   ground cinnamon
Pinch of grated nutmeg
Pinch of salt
20g caster sugar
2 eggs, beaten
80g butter, softened
   and cut into
   small pieces

1. Dissolve the sugar in the hot water in a jug or bowl and cool for a few moments.

2. Sprinkle in the yeast. Stir and allow to go frothy; this will take about 10 minutes.

3. Sift the flour, spices and salt together in a bowl if using a hand mixer and stir in the sugar. Put in the food processor if using.

4. Beat the eggs into the yeast mixture (use a hand mixer if not using a processor) and gradually add to the flour while the processor is on its lowest setting. Scrape the mixture from down the sides and mix for 2–3 minutes; this will knead the dough. Add a little more flour if it is too sticky.

5. When it has turned into a smooth dough, add the butter and mix in with the pulse action until the butter is fully blended.

6. Place the dough in an oiled bowl and cover. Leave in a cool place for 2–3 hours, or overnight in the fridge.

7. Butter a loaf or brioche tin.

8. Knock back the dough and knead it lightly for a minute. Place the dough in the prepared tin and leave to prove in a warm place for about 40 minutes, or until it has doubled in size.

9. Preheat the oven to 200°C/gas mark 6. Brush the top of the loaf with an egg-and-milk glaze if you like a shiny top.

10. Bake for 25–30 minutes until dark golden brown.

11. Remove from the tin immediately and cool on a wire rack.

12. When cool, slice and serve with butter and/or your favourite preserve, of you can slice it and fry the slices in butter. While frying, sprinkle with a little brown sugar.

Hot Cross Buns

These Easter buns are easy to make, and are best eaten warm or toasted.

Makes 10–12

450g strong white flour
  (or half white and half
  wholemeal)
1 level teaspoon salt
1–2 teaspoon
  mixed spice
1 x 7g sachet fast-action
  dried yeast
100g golden caster sugar
100g currants
50g candied mixed peel
Zest of 1 lemon
250ml warm milk
80g melted butter
1–2 tablespoons
  honey or golden
  syrup, to glaze

1. Sift the flour, salt and spice together into a large mixing bowl. Stir in the yeast, then the sugar.

2. Put the fruit and peel into a bowl and stir in the lemon zest.

3. Stir the fruit into the flour.

4. Make a well in the centre and pour in the milk and melted butter. Mix thoroughly with a wooden spoon.

5. Use your hands to knead the dough for 10 minutes.

6. Lightly oil a baking sheet. Break off small pieces of dough about the size of a small tangerine and knead each into a smooth ball. Place on the baking sheet, then flatten slightly with your hand.

7. Cover and prove for 35–40 minutes in a warm place. Preheat the oven to 200°C/gas mark 6.

8. Just before baking, use a very sharp knife to cut a cross into the top of each bun, or if you wish to be even more traditional, make a stiff pastry using 100g plain white flour mixed with 4–5 teaspoons of cold water. Roll out and cut into 24 little strips to make the crosses on top of the buns. Use water to moisten where the pastry will go and place the strips carefully on the top.

9. Bake for 15–20 minutes. Lift out of the oven, and while they are still hot, brush with honey or syrup to glaze.

10. Serve warm cut in half with butter.

Saffron Bread

This is also traditional Easter bread, served spread with butter.

Makes 1 medium-sized loaf

Tip of a teaspoon of
  saffron threads
140ml boiling water
450g strong white flour
½ level teaspoon salt
1 x 7g sachet
  fast-action yeast
50g golden
  caster sugar
120g sultanas
50g chopped
  mixed peel
100g butter
130ml milk
1 egg, beaten

1. Put the saffron in a small heatproof jug and pour in the boiling water. Leave for 2 hours.

2. Sift the flour and salt together into a large bowl. Stir in the yeast, sugar and dried fruit.

3. Melt the butter in a pan with the milk until it is just hot, then mix with the saffron water.

4. Make a well in the flour mixture and pour in the warm liquid and two-thirds of the egg; use the rest to glaze the top of the loaf.

5. Mix well with a wooden spoon until everything is combined, then leave for 20 minutes in a warm place.

6. Knead the dough for 10 minutes on a work surface dusted lightly with flour.

7. Grease a loaf tin large enough to hold the dough when doubled in size. Put the kneaded dough in the tin, cover with a tea towel and leave to prove in a warm place for about 30 minutes. Preheat the oven to 200°C/gas mark 6.

8. Brush the top with the rest of the egg and bake for 35–40 minutes; if after 20 minutes the bread is browning too quickly, turn the heat down to 190°C/gas mark 5 for the rest of the baking time.

9. Remove from the tin and cool on a rack. Allow to cool completely before slicing.

Oven-baked Doughnuts

Doughnuts are usually fried yeasted batter, but in this recipe they are baked, filled with jam and rolled in caster sugar. This lighter dough is unsuitable for hand-kneading, so it is beaten with a wooden spoon for about 4 minutes after combining.

Makes about 8

450g plain white flour
1 level teaspoon salt
1 x 7g sachet
   fast-action yeast
50g golden caster sugar
200ml milk
100g butter
2 eggs
Jam, for the filling; we like
   raspberry, but just
   choose your favourite
Melted butter, for
   brushing over
   the doughnuts
Caster sugar, for dusting
   over the finished
   doughnuts

1. Sift the flour and salt together into a large mixing bowl. Stir in the yeast and the sugar.

2. Warm the milk and butter in a pan over a very low heat. When the butter has melted, remove from the heat. Check that the milk is fairly warm (but not hot) before adding it to the flour.

3. Make a well in the flour and add the milk and beaten eggs. Mix everything together well with a wooden spoon.

4. Beat the mixture for 4 minutes. If it is too runny, sift in a little more flour as you beat. The mixture should be firm enough to handle.

5. Cover with a tea towel and leave in a warm place to prove for 20 minutes.

6. Lightly oil a baking tray. Roll out the dough using a rolling pin or flatten it down with your hands until it is about 6–7mm deep.

7. Using a sharp knife, cut the dough into squares measuring about 7cm. Put about a third of a teaspoon of jam in the centre and fold up the sides around it until it is sealed in.

8. Brush the entire surface of each doughnut with melted butter and place them on the baking tray, sealed edges down. Allow each one to touch the next. Brush the whole surface of the doughnuts again with melted butter. Cover, then leave to prove for 30 minutes in a warm place.

9. Preheat the oven to 200°C/gas mark 6.

10. Bake for about 20–25 minutes until golden brown. Allow to cool on the tray.

11. When cool, separate each doughnut and roll it in sugar. If you prefer, use icing sugar rather than caster to coat the doughnuts.

Savarin

This is like a large rum baba and is delicious topped with fresh fruit and nuts. It makes an excellent dessert.

Makes 1 large cake

110g plain white flour
½ level teaspoon salt
½ x 7g sachet
　fast-action yeast
2 tablespoons golden
　caster sugar
60ml warm milk
2 eggs
50g melted butter

For the syrup
100g caster sugar
50ml fruit juice or water
1 tablespoon rum
　or brandy

1. Sift the flour and salt together. Stir in the yeast and sugar.

2. Make a well in the centre of the dry ingredients, add the milk and eggs and beat into the flour vigorously. Continue beating for about 4 minutes. The dough should become smooth and elastic.

3. Lightly oil a ring tin and dust it with flour. Place the dough in the tin and leave to prove in a warm place until it has doubled in size.

4. Preheat the oven to 200°C/gas mark 6.

5. Bake the savarin for 20–30 minutes, or until golden brown.

6. Leave to cool in the tin for 15 minutes while you make the syrup.

7. Put the sugar and juice (or water) in a small pan over a low heat and stir gently until the sugar dissolves. Bring to the boil, then turn down the heat and simmer for a few minutes until the syrup thickens slightly.

8. Stir in the brandy or rum and allow to cool a little.

9. Turn the savarin out of the tin and onto a serving plate. Prick the sponge all over with a skewer. Drizzle the syrup over the entire surface, allow to soak in and repeat.

10. Leave to cool completely, then serve filled with fresh fruit and nuts as you wish. Serve with fresh cream.

Filling ideas
• Halved black and green grapes sprinkled with a little icing sugar

• Summer fruit mixture drizzled with liqueur or fruit syrup

• A small can of mandarin oranges, drained of most of the juice

• Dried fruit mixture soaked in orange juice and a tablespoon of Cointreau

Stollen

This Austrian fruit loaf is one of my particular favourites, due to its marzipan centre. It is a rich, filling addition to our table at Christmas, ideal to serve with coffee or a glass of port. For a little extra luxury, soak the fruit for three to four hours in three tablespoons of brandy before making the stollen.

380g plain flour
½ teaspoon salt
1 level teaspoon
  ground cinnamon
A little grated nutmeg
80g golden caster sugar
15g dried yeast mixed
  with 3 tablespoons
  warm milk and
  ½ teaspoon sugar
250ml warm milk
250g butter, melted
100g each raisins
  and currants
50g mixed candied peel
50g sultanas
50g chopped
  glacé cherries
50g flaked or
  chopped almonds
400g marzipan
Icing sugar,
  for dusting

1. Sift the flour, salt and spices into a large mixing bowl. Stir in the sugar.

2. Pour the 250ml of warm milk into the yeast mixture and stir in the melted butter.

3. Stir all the fruit into the flour mixture and make a well in the centre. Pour in the milk and yeast mixture. Stir with a wooden spoon until everything is combined.

4. Use your hands to knead the mixture for 3–4 minutes, then leave it to prove in a warm place for 30 minutes.

5. Keep the dough in the bowl and add a little flour, then knead for 5 minutes.

6. Divide the mixture into 2 equal parts. Transfer one to a floured work surface and press or roll it flat until it measures about 30cm x 20cm. Form the marzipan into a long roll to fit the dough with a couple of centimetres to spare and moisten the edges with water.

7. Flatten or roll the second section of dough to equal the size of the first. Place on top of the other and seal the edges around the marzipan. The stollen should look like a flattened log.

8. Place on an oiled baking sheet and leave to prove for 25–30 minutes.

9. Preheat the oven to 200°C/gas mark 6.

10. Bake for 25–30 minutes, then allow it to cool for 10 minutes. Brush with melted butter and dust with plenty of icing sugar.

SWEET AND TEA BREADS
My Notes

13
Making Pastry

Many people say they cannot make pastry, but following some helpful rules will make the process easier. Each type of pastry produces a different style and consistency, so each needs a slightly different approach. Apart from shortcrust pastry there are:

Types of pastry

Puff pastry was a very complicated affair when I was learning to cook, but it is a much quicker process now. It can be made light and airy simply by rubbing in all the butter, then rolling out the dough and folding. I top most of my savoury pies with puff pastry because it yields such a light finish.

Hot-water-crust pastry is closely associated with raised pork and meat pies. It gives a doughy finish to the pie on the inside that soaks up the meat juices so well, yet remains crispy and firm on the outside.

Choux pastry is used to make chocolate eclairs and profiteroles. With a little know-how, you can make these pastries at home at a fraction of what they cost in the shops.

Suet-crust pastry is the easiest pastry of all to make, and is used in hearty steak-and-kidney puddings or apple dumplings.

Sweet-crust pastry or *pâté sucre* is used to make sweet flans and pastries and is ideal for chocolate tarts.

Yeasted pastry is used for croissants and Danish pastries. It is light and rich, and with a little careful preparation, makes wonderful breakfast pastries.

Storing pastry

All types of shortcrust and puff pastry freeze well: simply wrap them in cling film, put in a freezer bag, seal and label with the date. Thaw completely in the wrapping before using. You may also make pastry two days in advance, wrap it in cling film and store in the fridge until you're ready to use it.

Shortcrust Pastry

This is the pastry most commonly used for topping pies and making slices, tarts and quiches. You can also use half wholemeal and half white flour in this recipe if you wish.

> **Tips for successful shortcrust pastry**
> • Keep all ingredients as cool as possible. Make sure the fat is very cold – straight from the fridge – and the water is ice-cold.
> • Cut the fat into small pieces and put in the fridge to cool.
> • Roll out the pastry quickly to the required thickness; too much rolling makes pastry heavy.

300g plain flour
½ level teaspoon salt
75g butter, cut into small pieces
75g lard, cut into small pieces
2 tablespoons cold water (more if necessary)

1. Sift the flour and salt into the bowl – be sure to lift the sieve up as high as possible so that the flour gets a really good airing.

2. Add both the fats and begin to rub the fat into the flour. If the fat softens too much in the process, put it back in the fridge for 10 minutes before continuing.

3. Keep rubbing in until the mixture looks like breadcrumbs. Keep it light; if your hands get hot, run your wrists under cold water, dry them and keep going. This stage may be done in the food processor.

4. Add a tablespoon of water and mix it in with a knife; the pastry should start to form clumps. Add the other tablespoon of water and mix it in the same way.

5. Bring the pastry together with your hands as lightly and quickly as possible. Don't be tempted to knead the pastry as it will end up tough and inedible.

6. When you can form the dough into a smooth ball, wrap it in cling film and put it in the fridge to cool for at least 30 minutes before use.

Variation
If using a food processor, sift the flour and salt together before pouring it into the processor. Add the butter and whizz the machine on its lowest setting until the mixture looks like breadcrumbs. Trickle in the water as it whizzes; as soon as the dough forms a ball, stop and remove it from the processor. Follow step 6 as in the regular recipe.

Rich Shortcrust Pastry

This is especially good for making mince pies at Christmas. The pastry melts in the mouth and also keeps fresh for longer.

300g plain flour
½ level teaspoon salt
170g butter
1 egg, beaten (or enough
    water to bind)

1. Sift the flour and salt into the bowl – be sure to lift the sieve up as high as possible so that the flour gets a really good airing.

2. Add the butter and begin to rub it into the flour. If the butter softens too much in the process, put it back in the fridge for 10 minutes before continuing.

3. Keep rubbing in until the mixture looks like breadcrumbs. Keep it light; if your hands get hot, run your wrists under cold water, dry them and keep going. This stage may be done in the food processor.

4. Add enough egg, a spoonful at a time, to bring the dough together, or use water.

5. Bring the pastry together with your hands as lightly and quickly as possible. Don't be tempted to knead the pastry as it will end up tough and inedible.

6. When you can form the dough into a smooth ball, wrap it in cling film and put it in the fridge to cool for at least 30 minutes before use.

Variations
• Add 50g caster sugar to the dry ingredients if you want a sweet pastry.

• Add 25g cocoa powder to the dry ingredients for chocolate pastry.

• Add 30g ground almonds or hazelnuts to the dry ingredients and stir them in well before adding the fat.

• Add and stir in well 1 tablespoon each of chopped chives and parsley and a ½ teaspoon fresh thyme leaves after rubbing in the butter. This makes an unusual crust for cheese and onion or cheese and potato pies.

Cheese Crust Pastry

This is delicious when wrapped around vegetables – and it makes a delicious apple pie.

120g plain white flour
100g wholemeal flour
½ level teaspoon salt,
    optional, as the
    cheese contains salt
50g butter, cut into
    cubes and chilled
    until needed
60g lard, cut into cubes
    and chilled until needed
100g mature
    Cheddar, grated
5–6 teaspoons water

1. To make the pastry, sieve the flours and salt (if using) together in a large mixing bowl.

2. Rub in the chilled fats until the mixture looks like breadcrumbs.

3. Stir in the cheese.

4. Add 2 tablespoons of cold water and stir in with a knife. Combine the mixture lightly with the fingers and add an extra teaspoon of water if the mixture is too dry. The dough must be soft but not sticky.

5. Chill for 20 minutes before using.

Easy Puff Pastry

Be very gentle with this when rolling it out so that you don't allow any of the air to escape.

225g plain flour
½ teaspoon salt
180g butter, straight
    from the fridge
80–100ml cold water

1. Sift the flour and salt into a bowl.

2. Add the butter in a whole block and cut it into the flour with a knife until the pieces are about 1cm in size. Alternatively, put the butter in the freezer for 1 hour, remove and grate, then stir it into the flour.

3. Stir in the water and bring the ingredients together with the knife; only use your hands at the very last minute to make a soft dough.

4. Dust your work surface with flour and roll out the pastry into a rectangle about 3 times as long as it is wide.

5. Fold the top third over to the centre, then the bottom third over the top and seal the edges.

6. Turn the pastry so that one sealed edge is next to you. Roll out into another rectangle and fold and seal in the same way.

7. Do this twice more, then leave it to rest for 30 minutes before using.

Hot-water Crust Pastry

I have tried to make this in a food processor, but it is much easier to mix it together with a wooden spoon because you can see the stiffness of the dough more easily.

500g plain flour
1 level teaspoon salt
220ml boiling water
220g lard

1. Sieve the flour and salt together into a mixing bowl and make a well in the centre.

2. Pour the boiling water into a heatproof jug and add the fat. Allow it to melt into the water, then stir this into the flour with a wooden spoon.

3. Bring together with your hands to form a smooth dough.

Suet Crust Pastry

This makes enough for a large pudding or jam roly-poly.

220g self-raising flour
½–1 level teaspoon salt
110g suet
Cold water to mix

1. Sieve the flour and salt together. Stir in the suet.

2. Mix in the water a teaspoon at a time until the dough is soft but pliable.

3. Knead gently to bring the dough together.

Choux Pastry

You can use water or milk as the liquid, but I find water makes a lighter pastry.

70g plain flour
150ml water or milk
50g butter
2 eggs

1. Sieve the flour into a bowl.

2. Put the water or milk and butter in a pan over a low heat and heat gently until the butter melts.

3. Bring to the boil, then remove from the heat and stir in the flour quickly with a wooden spoon.

4. Return the pan to the heat and cook for a few minutes, stirring all the time until the mixture comes away from the sides.

5. Cool for 2 minutes, then beat in the eggs gradually. The dough should be thick enough for piping but not too stiff. Use immediately.

Sweet-crust Pastry

This light, sweet crust is ideal for sweet tarts and flans. It can be made well in advance of using and can keep for two days in the fridge.

200g plain flour
100g butter
70g golden caster sugar
1 egg

1. Sift the flour into a mixing bowl and rub in the butter until the mixture resembles breadcrumbs.

2. Stir in the sugar.

3. Beat the egg and make a well in the flour. Add half of the egg; this is best done using a spoon. Stir in with a knife, and add another small amount of egg if the dough is too dry.

4. Bring the dough together with your fingers using light, gentle movements. Use a food processor if you wish.

5. When the dough is ready, flatten it into a round and wrap it in cling film.

6. Leave to rest for at least 30 minutes before using.

7. When you come to roll out the pastry, do this between layers of cling film. Roll gently until the pastry fits the tin. Sweet-crust pastry should be rolled as thinly as possible – that's why it's easier to do this using cling film.

MAKING PASTRY
My Notes

14
Using Pastry

Homemade pastry can be used in almost unlimited delicious recipes, both sweet and savoury. Having made-up pastry to hand is always worthwhile, because you can combine it with a small number of ingredients to make many filling meals very quickly. For example, a small package of meat and a few vegetables can be transformed into a hearty, mouth-watering pie for a family of four without costing the earth. And if you need a fast dessert or pudding, a tart can be rustled up in no time.

Sausage and Apple Pies

These are little individual pies, but you can make a larger pie in a deep pie dish; I use muffin tins (the bun tin is a little too small). They are great for buffet lunches or picnics served with a salad, and are delicious served both hot or cold.

If you have problems getting good-quality sausage meat, buy 500g pork sausages and remove the skins. You can also make your own sausage meat using 500g finely minced pork combined with 150g fresh breadcrumbs, ½ teaspoon salt, ¼–½ teaspoon ground black pepper, ½ teaspoon chopped sage and 120ml water. Mix well with your hands, cover and leave overnight; if using this, you won't need any more seasoning.

Makes 6–8 pies

500g good pork
  sausage meat
Black pepper
Salt to taste
½ teaspoon chopped
  fresh sage
500g shortcrust pastry
  (see page 184)
2 large Bramley apples,
  peeled, cored
  and sliced

1. Preheat the oven to 180°C/gas mark 4.

2. Put the sausage meat in a bowl and mix in some freshly ground black pepper and salt to taste. Add the sage and combine with your hands.

3. Grease a muffin tin. Roll out the pastry and cut out rounds to fit the tin compartments. Save some pastry for the lids.

4. Put 2 slices of apple in the bottom of each pastry, then a spoonful of sausage meat. Repeat this but finish with an extra layer of apple.

5. Put on a pastry lid, moistening the edges with water so that they stick together. Make a slit in the top to allow the steam to escape. If desired, brush the tops of the pies with beaten egg to give them a shiny finish before they are baked.

6. Bake for 35–40 minutes, or until the pastry is golden.

7. Allow to cool in the tins for 15–20 minutes before removing. They will still be hot for serving but easier to remove.

Variation
Add a layer of Lancashire or similar crumbly cheese in the centre of the pies, between the apple and sausage meat.

Kipper Quiche

This tasty flan with a smoky flavour can be served with salad and crusty bread. You can make either one large flan case or four individual ones.

Serves 4

250g shortcrust pastry
 (see page 184)
Approximately 200g
 kipper fillets
2 eggs
300ml milk
1 tablespoon of fresh
 or 1 level teaspoon
 dried parsley

1. Preheat the oven to 200°C/gas mark 6 and grease a 20cm flan tin or 4 small ones.

2. Roll out the pastry to 1cm thick and of a size to fit and line the prepared tin. Cut a piece of greaseproof paper into a circle about 4cm larger than the tin; put this over the pastry shell and weigh it down with baking beads or dried beans. Bake in the oven for 15 minutes.

3. Prepare the kippers by skinning them and checking for any bones. Leave the flesh in bite-size pieces.

4. When the pastry is set, spread the kippers over the base.

5. Whisk the eggs with the milk and pour over the kippers.

6. Sprinkle the top with the parsley.

7. Put the quiche on a baking sheet and bake for about 30 minutes, or until the filling has set.

Cornish Pasties

The great thing about pasties like these is that they will keep warm for at least an hour after baking if you wrap them in a tea towel. The potatoes should be cut into thin, crisp-like slices rather than diced, but if you want to dice them, make sure they are very small.

Makes 4 large pasties

500g shortcrust pastry
(see page 184)
4 medium potatoes,
sliced thinly
1 onion, chopped
120g swede, diced
Salt and white pepper
to taste
350g best braising
steak, cut into very
small chunks
50g butter
1 egg yolk mixed with
3 tablespoons milk

1. Cut the pastry into 4 equal portions. Roll out each section to the size of a small dinner plate.

2. Combine the potato, onion and swede in a bowl and season with salt and pepper.

3. Put a pile of the vegetables in the centre of the pastry circles and pile a quarter of the meat on top of each one.

4. Dot the filling with butter. Preheat the oven to 220°C/gas mark 7.

5. Dampen the edges with water and fold to make a semi-circle. Turn the edges up and over to seal, then stand them up so that the sealed edge is at the top. Pinch and crimp the pastry.

6. Brush with the beaten egg and milk mixture and bake on a greased baking sheet for 10 minutes, then turn the heat down to 170°C/gas mark 3 and bake for a further 35–40 minutes. Cool slightly if eating straight away.

Double Gloucester Cheese and Asparagus Flan

Creamy Double Gloucester cheese goes really well with asparagus. The UK doesn't have a long asparagus season, and when it is getting scarce, this is a good way to make a little go a long way. This flan is best served with a green salad and some cherry tomatoes.

Serve 6

200g shortcrust pastry (see page 184)
100g Double Gloucester cheese, grated
6–8 asparagus spears, steamed or boiled for 3 minutes and cut into 2cm lengths
1 small red onion, chopped finely
2 eggs
1 level teaspoon dry mustard powder
280ml single cream
Salt and freshly ground black pepper, to taste

1. Grease a 20cm flan tin and preheat the oven to 200°C/gas mark 6.

2. Roll out the pastry to fit the tin, giving a little extra to allow for shrinkage. Line the tin with pastry, place a sheet of baking paper on the base and weigh it down with baking beans. Put the tin on a baking sheet and bake it 'blind' in the oven for 15–20 minutes. Remove from the oven and set aside for the filling.

3. Reduce the temperature of the oven to 180°C/gas mark 4.

4. Sprinkle half of the cheese over the base of the flan, then scatter the asparagus and onion on top. Finish with the rest of the cheese.

5. Beat the eggs, mustard powder and the cream together and season with salt and black pepper – remember, though, the cheese is salty. Pour the egg and cream mixture over the cheese.

6. Put back on the baking sheet and bake for 30–35 minutes, or until the egg mixture has set and the top has become golden brown.

7. Allow to cool for 10 minutes before slicing.

Leek Tart

This is wonderful as a buffet dish or served with summer salads.

Serves 4–6

200g shortcrust pastry
  (see page 184)
80g butter
700g leeks, washed,
  trimmed and
  sliced thinly
120ml double cream
Salt and pepper to taste
A little grated nutmeg
80g mature Cheddar

1. Preheat the oven to 190°C/gas mark 5. Grease a 20cm flan tin.

2. Roll out the pastry to line the tin, place a sheet of baking paper on the base and weigh it down with baking beans. Put the tin on a baking sheet and bake it 'blind' in the oven for about 15 minutes.

3. Melt the butter in a frying pan and fry the leeks gently until tender.

4. Stir in the cream and season with salt, pepper and nutmeg. Remove from the heat.

5. When the pastry shell is ready (it won't be fully cooked; just set), pour in the leek mixture and sprinkle the cheese on top.

6. Bake for 25–30 minutes, or until the filling turns golden brown. Serve hot or cold.

Stargazy Pie

This pie is not for the faint-hearted: you'll know exactly what has gone into it because the fish are staring up at you! But it tastes good, and is great fun to serve to friends and family.

Serves 6

12 large sardines or
  8 pilchards
8 rashers of streaky
  bacon, chopped
3 eggs, softly boiled
1 large onion,
  chopped finely
1 tablespoon fresh,
  chopped parsley
450g shortcrust pastry
  (see page 184)
Juice of 1 lemon
Salt and pepper to taste
Milk to glaze

1. Clean and bone the fish and season the insides. Remove the heads of all but 3 of the pilchards or 4 of the sardines.

2. Preheat the oven to 180°C/gas mark 4.

3. Combine the bacon, eggs, onion and parsley in a bowl.

4. Grease a large pie dish and roll out half of the pastry in a thin disc. Line the dish with the pastry.

5. Put a little of the bacon mixture inside each fish and place the headless fish on the pastry in a circle, tails in the centre. Pile the rest of the bacon mixture over and around the fish.

6. Pour the lemon juice over the fish and season to taste.

7. Roll out the other half of the pastry and wet the edges of the pie before placing the lid on top of the fish.

8. Make 3–4 slits in the pastry big enough to contain a head and place each 'headed' fish in a pastry slit.

9. Glaze the top of the pie with milk and bake for 40 minutes, or until the pie is golden in colour. Serve hot.

Cheese and Vegetable Pie with a Herb Crust

Very tasty and filling, this is almost a ratatouille pie. You can add other vegetables of your choice at various times of the year: carrots and turnips, beetroot and leeks. Alter the cheese to fit in with whatever you have; Cheshire or Red Leicester make good alternatives.

Serves 6

30g butter or oil
1 onion, chopped
1 large red pepper, diced
Half a small
  aubergine, diced
2 courgettes,
  diced or sliced
200g open-cap
  mushrooms
2 garlic cloves, crushed
3 tablespoons
  tomato purée
Salt and black pepper
  to taste
300g herb pastry
  (see page 185,
  variations)
2 large, fresh
  tomatoes, sliced
150g mozzarella,
  cubed or grated
150g mature
  Cheddar, grated

1. Preheat the oven to 190°C/gas mark 5. Grease a deep 20cm pie dish.

2. Melt the butter or heat the oil in a frying pan and fry the onion and pepper until soft.

3. Add the other vegetables, mushrooms and garlic and fry gently for 3-4 minutes. Stir in the tomato purée. Season to taste. Remove from the heat and cool.

4. Cut off a third of the pastry for the top of the pie and roll out the rest to line the pie dish.

5. Lay the tomato slices over the base of the pie and season with a little more salt and pepper if you wish.

6. Spread the mozzarella over the tomatoes and cover with the cooked vegetables. Sprinkle the Cheddar over the whole filling.

7. Roll out the lid and moisten the edges of the pastry. Lay the lid on top and press down the edges. Crimp with your finger and thumb to seal well and cut 3 slashes in the lid.

8. Bake for 30 minutes, then turn down the oven to 180°C/gas mark 4 and bake 10–15 minutes more, or until the top is a deep golden brown. Serve hot with potato salad, lettuce and cucumber.

Sweet Pumpkin Pie

This is a real autumn winner, one you will want to make time and time again. It is very easy and tastes wonderful. Steam or roast the pumpkin until just soft, then mash or purée it in a food processor.

Serves 8

300g shortcrust pastry
    (see page 184)
2 large eggs
100g soft brown sugar
Pinch of salt
1 level teaspoon
    ground cinnamon
Pinch of grated nutmeg
500g pumpkin
    flesh, cooked
280ml double cream
50ml milk
Icing sugar, for dusting

1. Preheat the oven to 200°C/gas mark 6. Grease a 23cm loose-bottomed flan tin.

2. Roll out the pastry and line the tin.

3. Beat the eggs, sugar, salt and spices together in a large bowl.

4. Add the pumpkin, cream and milk and fold everything in together.

5. Pour the pumpkin mixture into the prepared pastry shell.

6. Bake for 15 minutes at 200°C/gas mark 6, then turn down the heat to 190°C/gas mark 5 and bake for 35–40 minutes.

7. Allow to cool in the tin on a cooling rack for 30 minutes, then transfer to a serving plate and dust with icing sugar. Serve with cream or crème fraîche.

Almond Slice

This was my mum's recipes. She would make a batch of slices: this one, a coconut slice and some flapjacks. They would last all week, she said. They very rarely did, however – especially when my friends came to call!

Makes 10–12 portions

300g shortcrust pastry
(see page 184)
3 tablespoons raspberry
or cherry jam
120g caster sugar
80g icing sugar
150g ground almonds
50g semolina
½–1 teaspoon
almond extract
1 whole egg, plus
the yolk from the
separated white
below, beaten
1 egg white, whisked
until very foamy
but not stiff
50g flaked almonds

1. Preheat the oven to 200°C/gas mark 6. Grease a rectangular baking tin measuring about 18cm x 28cm.

2. Roll out the pastry to fit the tin and spread the base with the jam of your choice.

3. Put the caster sugar into a large mixing bowl and sift in the icing sugar. Stir in the ground almonds and semolina.

4. Beat the almond extract into the beaten egg and pour this mixture over the dry ingredients. Stir in.

5. Fold in the egg white and spoon the mixture over the top of the jam.

6. Scatter the flaked almonds evenly over the top.

7. Bake for 25–30 minutes until the pastry is golden around the outside and the filling is set and crispy.

8. Allow to cool in the tin for 30 minutes, then cut into slices.

9. Use a fish slice to transfer the slices to a cooling rack to cool completely before storing in an airtight tin.

Mince Pie with Apple Slices

If time is short (and whose isn't at Christmas?) remember that making one large mince pie is easier than making a lot of small ones, and you use less pastry. Use rich shortcrust pastry for this special dessert. Of course, it can be eaten at any time of the year – not just Christmas.

Serves 8

300g rich shortcrust pastry (see page 185)
400g mincemeat,
1 large Bramley apple, peeled, cored and sliced and left in cold water containing a couple of teaspoons of lemon juice

1. Preheat the oven to 200°C/gas mark 6. Grease a 20cm deep pie dish.

2. Cut and reserve one-third of the pastry for the top of the pie and roll out the rest to line the pie dish.

3. Spread the mincemeat evenly over the pastry.

4. Lay the apple slices in the mincemeat.

5. Roll out the lid and moisten the edges with water. Place the lid on the top of the pie and seal the edges. Cut three slashes in the top of the pie.

6. Bake for 25–30 minutes, or until the pastry is deep golden in colour. If the crust is browning too quickly, turn the heat down to 180°C/gas mark 4 for the last 10 minutes of baking time.

Chorley Cakes

You can make one large or six small cakes with this recipe. If you make a big one you can simply cut slices as you need them.

Makes 1 large or 6 small ones

50g butter
30g soft brown sugar
1 level teaspoon
   mixed spice
Grated zest of 1 orange
   and 1 lemon
150g currants
300g ordinary or rich
   shortcrust pastry
   (see pages 184–5)

For the topping
1 egg white
2 teaspoons
   caster sugar

1. Preheat the oven to 200°C/gas mark 6. Grease a large baking sheet.

2. Beat the butter, sugar, spice and fruit zest together until light and fluffy.

3. Add the currants and beat into the creamed mixture.

4. Roll out the pastry either into 1 large or 6 small rounds.

5. Spoon the filling into the centre of the round(s) and bring up the edges to cover. Pinch and seal the edges and lightly roll with a rolling pin to flatten into a round shape.

6. Place on the prepared baking sheet and brush with the egg white. Sprinkle with the caster sugar.

7. Bake for 20 minutes for small ones or 30–35 minutes for a large one.

8. Serve warm or cold – and with custard if you wish.

Crunchy Cornflake Slice

This unusual slice can be served on its own or with custard or cream.

Makes 8 servings

250g ordinary or rich
  shortcrust pastry
  (see pages 184–5)
5–6 tablespoons jam
  of your choice
60g butter
60g golden
  caster sugar
2 tablespoons
  golden syrup
180g cornflakes,
  lightly crushed

1. Preheat the oven to 200°C/gas mark 6. Grease a 20cm loose-bottomed flan tin.

2. Roll out the pastry to fit the tin and chill it for 15 minutes. Line the pastry with some baking paper, put some baking beans on top and bake it 'blind' for 25 minutes.

3. Spread the base of the flan with the jam.

4. In a pan, melt the butter with the sugar and golden syrup over a low heat.

5. When everything is mixed and melted together, stir in the cornflakes and spread the mixture carefully over the jam.

6. Bake for 5 minutes only, then leave to cool completely before slicing.

Treacle Tart

A treat that is best served warm with vanilla ice cream.

Serves 6

200g ordinary or rich
   shortcrust pastry
   (see pages 184–5)
80g fresh breadcrumbs
230g golden syrup
Grated zest and
   juice of 1 lemon

1. Preheat the oven to 190°C/gas mark 5.

2. Grease a 20cm round flan tin or pie plate. Roll out the pastry quite thinly and line the tin with it. Keep any trimmings for the top.

3. Spread the breadcrumbs over the pastry base.

4. Warm the syrup with the lemon zest and juice in a small pan over a low heat or in a heatproof jug in the microwave until just warm and runny. Stir, then pour the syrup evenly over the breadcrumbs.

5. Roll out the pastry trimmings and cut into thin equal strips – 6 should do: 3 for each direction. Moisten the edge of the tart with water. Twist each strip, then press each edge firmly into the pastry rim.

6. Bake for about 25–30 minutes until the pastry is deep golden brown and the filling is set.

Easy Banoffi Pie

Using condensed milk for the base of this pie makes it a very easy treat. But do be very careful when opening the can after the cooking time, as the inside is ultra-hot and may spurt out; hold a tea towel over the can for the first incision with the tin opener. The condensed milk will have become runny, creamy caramel.

1x 400g can
  condensed milk
200g sweet-crust pastry
  (see page 188)
3 bananas
300ml whipping cream
1 level tablespoon
  cocoa powder
1 level tablespoon icing
  sugar, optional

1. Stand the can of condensed milk in a pan of simmering water and simmer vigorously for 2 hours.

2. Preheat the oven to 200°C/gas mark 6. Grease a 20cm pie dish.

3. Roll out the pastry to fit the pie dish, line it with baking parchment, scatter baking beans on the base and bake it blind for 25 minutes, or until golden brown. Remove the baking paper and beans.

4. When the condensed milk is ready, remove it from the water and allow it to cool for 10 minutes. Open the can carefully and pour the contents over the cooked pastry base.

5. Slice the banana and press the pieces carefully into the condensed milk. Leave to cool completely.

6. Whip the cream and pile it on top of the pie.

7. Sieve the cocoa powder and icing sugar (if using) together over the top of the pie. Chill for 1 hour before serving.

Cherry and Frangipane Tart

Using the ground almond shortcrust pastry for this recipe makes it ultra-delicious.

Serves 8

250g almond pastry
  (see page 185,
  variations)
130g butter
130g golden caster sugar
2 eggs, beaten
130g ground almonds
20g plain flour
1 x 200g can black
  cherries, drained

1. Preheat the oven to 190°C/gas mark 5. Grease a 23cm fluted loose-bottomed tin.

2. Roll out the pastry to fit the tin, pressing it lightly into the flutes.

3. To make the frangipane, cream the butter and sugar together in a mixing bowl. Cream in the eggs gradually. Fold in the almonds and sift in the flour.

4. Spread the mixture evenly over the pastry base.

5. Press the cherries into the frangipane at regular intervals.

6. Bake for 45–50 minutes, or until the filling is golden brown on the top.

7. Cool for 20 minutes, then carefully remove the flan from the tin and serve with cream or ice cream.

Rich Chocolate Tart

A chocolate-lover's dream: this tart is rich and creamy without being too sweet – but you can always add a little more sugar if you prefer it sweeter.

Serves 8

200g chocolate pastry
(see page 185,
variations)
200g dark chocolate,
broken into pieces
100ml milk
280ml double cream
2 eggs
80g golden caster sugar

1. Preheat the oven to 200°C/gas mark 6. Grease a 20cm flan tin.

2. Roll out the pastry to fit the tin, line it with baking paper and scatter over some baking beans. Bake it 'blind' for 15 minutes. Remove the baking paper and beans and turn the oven temperature down to 150°C/gas mark 2.

3. Melt the chocolate in a heatproof bowl placed over simmering water. Use some of it to brush the pastry shell carefully.

4. Pour the milk and cream into a saucepan and bring to the boil. Remove from the heat straight away and pour carefully into the remaining chocolate.

5. Beat the eggs and sugar together and stir into the cream and chocolate mixture.

6. Pour the mixture into the pastry shell. Bake for about 40–45 minutes until the filling is set but still wobbles when you move it.

7. Allow to cool but don't chill it: it loses some of its flavour if served too cold.

Apple Pie with Cheddar Crust

A traditional apple pie with the added flavour of cheese pastry. Don't serve this with custard, however; cream is best.

Serves 6–8

300g cheese
   crust pastry
   (see page 186)
3 Bramley apples
1 tablespoon
   lemon juice
50ml water
3–4 tablespoons soft
   brown sugar

1. Preheat the oven to 190°C/gas mark 5. Grease a 20cm pie dish.

2. Reserve a third of the pastry for the top and roll the rest out to fit the prepared dish.

3. Peel, core and slice the apples. Drizzle them with lemon juice, put them into the pastry shell and sprinkle them with the brown sugar. If you wish to cook the apples, put them in a saucepan with the lemon juice, water and sugar and bring to the boil. Turn down the heat and simmer for 5 minutes. Allow to cool before spooning into the pastry shell.

4. Roll out the remaining pastry so that it just fits the top. Moisten the edges with water and press together to seal. Make 2 slits in the centre of the lid to allow the steam to escape.

5. Bake for 35–40 minutes, or until the pastry is deep golden in colour.

6. Serve hot or cold.

Raised Pork and Chicken Pie

This uses hot-water crust pastry. Using the chicken gives it a flavour variation, but if you prefer, you can substitute 500g diced pork instead.

500g hot-water crust
  pastry (see page 187)
500g minced pork
500g chicken thigh meat,
  cut into 1cm chunks
½ teaspoon dried sage
2 level teaspoons salt
White pepper to taste

1. Preheat the oven to 175°C/gas mark 3. Grease a 20cm round loose-bottomed or springform tin.

2. Roll out the cooled pastry to line the tin. It should be rolled slightly thicker than other pastry because it has to be cooked for longer.

3. Combine the meats with the sage, salt and pepper and stir everything well.

4. Press the meat down firmly into the pastry case and top with a lid. Seal the edges firmly and brush with an egg and milk glaze if you wish.

5. Place the tin on a baking sheet. It will catch any drips and make it easier to get the pie in and out of the oven.

6. Bake for 1½ hours, then test the centre with a knife; if it comes out clean, it's ready, but if not, bake for 15 minutes more, then test again.

7. Leave to cool in the tin, preferably overnight, so that the juices will firm up and the pie will be ready to slice.

Red Onion and Cream Cheese Tart

An easy, tasty tart that is perfect for parties and buffets.

Serves 8

300g puff pastry
(see page 186)
15g butter or olive oil
4 red onions,
sliced thinly
½ teaspoon fresh
thyme leaves
200g soft cream cheese
Salt and black pepper
to taste

1. Preheat the oven to 200°C/gas mark 6. Grease a baking tray.

2. Roll out the pastry until it measures about 25cm square and place it on the baking sheet. Prick the centre of the pastry, leaving a 3cm unpricked edge all round, and bake for 15 minutes until golden and risen round the edges.

3. Heat the oil or butter in a frying pan and fry the onion with the thyme for 15–20 minutes until soft.

4. Remove from the heat and stir in the cream cheese.

5. Spread the filling over the centre of the pastry case, and serve warm or cold.

Variation
Use 200g button mushrooms halved and fried in a little butter until the mushroom liquor has almost evaporated, then stir in 100g cream cheese with garlic and herbs. Spread over the baked pastry as before and serve warm.

Stow Pie

When I was a teenager, my family went on holiday to a wonderful little place on the River Severn called Haw Bridge. There in the pub on the banks of the river we ate Stow pies – a rich blend of beef and venison. I have never managed to find a basic recipe, but here is my version, made from memory, and it tastes very similar.

Serves 6

1 tablespoon
   sunflower oil
1 large onion,
   sliced thinly
400g lean braising beef,
   cut into chunks
700g venison,
   cut into chunks
550ml beef stock
   or water
100ml red wine
Salt and white pepper
   to taste
1 tablespoon
   cornflour mixed
   with 2 tablespoons
   cold water
300g puff pastry
   (see page 186)

1. Heat the oil in a frying pan and fry the onion until soft. Transfer to a large lidded pan.

2. Add the beef and venison to the lidded pan and fry gently until the meat is sealed all over.

3. Pour in the stock and wine and bring to the boil. Then turn down the heat and season as necessary. Put on the lid and simmer for 2½ hours.

4. Add the cornflour mixture and stir until it thickens.

5. Transfer the meat to a deep rectangular pie dish. If there is too much gravy, reserve some to serve later. Preheat the oven to 200°C/gas mark 6.

6. Roll out the pastry so that it just fits inside the pie dish – about 1cm thick – and place it on top of the meat. Cut 3 slits in the centre and bake for 20–25 minutes, or until the pastry has risen and looks flaky.

7. Serve immediately with creamed potatoes and a green vegetable. Don't forget to reheat any gravy you have saved!

Mutton Pie

You can use mutton or lamb for this recipe; just make sure the meat is well-trimmed of fat.

Serves 6

2 tablespoons oil
1kg mutton or lamb,
    cut into 2cm cubes
2 large onions, chopped
450g turnips, peeled
    and thickly sliced
1 level teaspoon dried
    or 1 rounded
    teaspoon freshly
    chopped rosemary
1 tablespoon
    chopped parsley
Salt and pepper to taste
300ml warm stock
    or water
1 tablespoon
    plain flour
225g puff pastry
    (see page 186)

1. Heat the oil in a large lidded pan and fry the meat and onions together for 4–5 minutes, turning everything so that the meat fries evenly.

2. Add the turnips and cook for 3 more minutes.

3. Add the herbs and season to taste.

4. Pour in the stock or water and stir. Allow to simmer, then cover and cook at simmering for 1½ hours. Check the liquid levels and add a little more if necessary.

5. Add the flour to 2 tablespoons of water and stir it into the meat mixture. Bring to the boil, stirring constantly, then turn down to simmering. Simmer for a further 15 minutes.

6. Preheat the oven to 200°C/gas mark 6.

7. Pour the pie filling into a deep pie dish. Allow the filling to cool for 10 minutes, or the pastry won't rise. Roll out the pastry to fit the top and cover the meat with it, making a slit in the centre for steam to escape.

8. Bake for 35–40 minutes until the pastry has risen and is golden and flaky. Serve immediately with boiled new potatoes and garden peas.

Rich Fish Pie

Most fish pie recipes have a potato topping, but this one uses puff pastry. It is easy to make, and I like it because it isn't too creamy. Serve with peas or green beans and fresh crusty bread or boiled potatoes.

800g fish fillets: whiting, haddock, salmon, pollack, etc.
200g large cooked prawns
½ teaspoon cayenne pepper
A little grated mace
50g butter
Salt and black pepper to taste
250ml fish stock
50ml white wine
1 tablespoon cornflour mixed with a little cold fish stock or water
2 tablespoons fresh chopped parsley
300g puff pastry (see page 186)

1. Preheat the oven to 200°C/gas mark 6. Butter a large, deep oval or rectangular pie dish.

2. Cut the fish into large chunks and put them in the dish. Add the prawns.

3. Blend the cayenne pepper and mace with the butter, then dot this all over the fish. Season to taste.

4. Put the stock and wine in a pan and bring to the boil. Stir in the cornflour mixture; don't worry if it is very thick – the fish juices will mingle with it while it is cooking.

5. Sprinkle the parsley over the fish and pour the stock evenly over the filling. Stir a little to make sure everything is evenly distributed.

6. Roll out the pastry and cover the filling with it. Make 3 cuts in the centre of the pastry to release steam.

7. Bake for 30–35 minutes. If the crust is browning too quickly, turn down the heat after 20 minutes to 190°C/gas mark 5.

Vanilla Slices

This is one of my great favourites from our local bakery: the vanilla custard filling is to die for! They won't tell me their secret, but this is close.

Makes 4

300g puff pastry
  (see page 186)
250ml vanilla pastry
  custard or
  crème pâtissière
  (see page 12)
100g icing sugar
Extra icing sugar,
  for dusting

1. Preheat the oven to 200°C/gas mark 6. Grease a baking sheet.

2. Roll out the pastry until it measures 20cm x 40cm; it should be quite thin. Lay it carefully on the baking sheet. The easiest way to do this is to rest it over the rolling pin and allow the rolling pin to carry it across to the baking sheet.

3. Prick the pastry all over, right to the edges. This means it won't rise much but will have the melt-in-the-mouth texture associated with good vanilla slices.

4. Bake for 15–20 minutes until golden brown. Allow to cool on the baking sheet. Dust the pastry as it is cooling with icing sugar.

5. When it is cool cut it into 4 rectangles. Sandwich 2 rectangles with a quarter of the custard filling. Be generous: it has to ooze out when you eat them!

6. Sift the icing sugar into a bowl and mix it with sufficient water to make a coating that is easy to use to top the slices. Don't spread this on the pastry; spoon it on, then gently smooth the top with a damp palette knife if necessary.

Variation
Use cream and a little strawberry jam as the filling: whip 200ml double cream until it holds its shape before spreading on 1 pastry half. Spread about a level teaspoon of strawberry jam on the other slice, then sandwich together. Top with icing as before.

Richmond Maids of Honour

These wonderfully satisfying little cakes were given their name by Henry Vlll, who found some ladies eating them in the gardens of Hampton Court. The King tasted one and christened them maids of honour. Two hundred years later the recipe was handed to a shopkeeper in Richmond upon Thames. They are very easy to make and are very similar to curd tarts.

Makes 14–16

220g cottage cheese
80g golden caster sugar
50g currants
Grated zest of 1 lemon
20g chopped almonds
1 egg, beaten
1 dessertspoon brandy
20g butter, melted
200g puff pastry
  (see page 186)
1 dessertspoon icing
  sugar, for dusting

1. Preheat the oven to 190°C/gas mark 5. Grease 16 holes of 2 x 12-hole bun tins.

2. Strain all the liquid from the cottage cheese and put it into a large bowl. Chop the curds with a knife and stir in the sugar, currants, lemon zest, chopped almonds, egg, brandy and butter. Stir everything well.

3. Roll out the pastry quite thinly and cut into circles that fit the tin holes. Make sure the pastry comes well up the sides of each hole.

4. Spoon the cheese mixture into the pastry cases until each is two-thirds full.

5. Bake for 20–25 minutes until the pastry and the top are golden brown.

6. Cool and dust with icing sugar.

SUET-CRUST PASTRY

This type of pastry is usually steamed rather than baked, but here is one recipe that is baked in the oven.

Suet Crusties

My mum made these as an alternative to dumplings. We ate them with all kinds of thick soups and stews, especially ones made with ham or bacon.

Makes 8

220g self-raising flour
½ teaspoon salt
½ teaspoon dry
 mustard powder
110g suet (I use
 vegetarian, but
 any will do)
Water to mix

1. Preheat the oven to 200°C/gas mark 6. Grease a baking sheet.

2. Sift the flour, salt and mustard powder together into a bowl. Stir in the suet.

3. Add 4 teaspoons of water and use a knife to mix the dough. Keep adding water a teaspoon at a time until a soft, but not too sticky, dough is formed.

4. Bring the dough together with your hands and transfer it to a floured surface.

5. Roll it out until the dough measures 2cm thick and is a rectangular shape.

6. Cut into 8 squares and place on the baking sheet.

7. Bake for about 20–30 minutes until golden and crispy. Serve warm with soups and stews.

Variation
Stir in 1 tablespoon fresh chopped herbs of your choice before mixing in the water.

Chocolate Cream Eclairs

These are filled with a rich chocolate custard. I had them in France when on holiday many years ago: they cost a fortune but were well worth it. They will only keep for 24 hours, however – but they usually don't last that long.

Makes 12 large cakes

I quantity choux pastry
(see page 187)
I quantity of chocolate
cream custard
(see page 12)
50g dark chocolate
50g icing sugar mixed
with a few teaspoons
cold water to make
a firm icing

*For the chocolate
topping*
100g dark chocolate
30g butter
30ml double cream

1. Preheat the oven to 200°C/gas mark 6. Grease a baking sheet.

2. Put the choux dough into a piping bag and pipe strips about 8cm long onto the baking sheet. Drizzle with a little water to help them rise. Bake for 20 minutes until puffed up and well risen.

3. Remove from the oven and release the steam by piercing each pastry with a darning needle. They will then stay crisp.

4. Cut each in half lengthways and fill with the chocolate cream custard.

5. Melt the chocolate in a bowl over a pan of hot water, then mix it into the icing sugar along with a knob of butter.

6. Spread some chocolate icing on each eclair.

For profiteroles
1. Pipe small blobs of the pastry onto a greased baking sheet and cook for 15 minutes at 200°C/gas mark 6.

2. Either split the profiteroles in half or use a cooking syringe to insert the cream into the centre of the choux puffs.

3. Pile them up a serving plate and drizzle melted chocolate all over the mountain of profiteroles.

For the chocolate topping
1. Put all the ingredients in a bowl over hot water and stir gently until all the chocolate has melted.

2. Use this to drizzle over the profiteroles.

3. Alternatively, melt 100g white chocolate with a knob of butter and drizzle this over the profiteroles.

Index